Tuath na Dromann

A History Of Cill Na Martra

by

Donal Murphy

© 2008 Donal Murphy

All rights reserved. No part of this publication may be reproduced in any form or by any means—graphic, electronic or mechanical, including photocopying, recording, taping or information storage and retrieval systems—without the prior written permission of the author.

ISBN: 978-1-906018-61-0

A CIP catalogue for this book is available from the National Library.

Published by Original Writing Ltd., Dublin, 2008.

Printed in Ireland by Cahills Printers Ltd

AN BROLLACH

As ní coitchend soilleir fon uile domhan in gach ionadh i mbí uaisle no onoir in gach aimsir da ttainicc riamh diaidh i ndiaidh nach ffuil ní as glórmaire, & is airmittnighe onoraighe (ar adhbharaibh iomdha) ina fios sendachta na senughdar, & eolas na naireach, & na nuasal ro bhádar ann isin aimsir rempo do thabhairt do chum solais ar dhaigh co mbeith aithentas, & eolas ag gach druing i ndeadhaidh aroile cionnas do chaithsiot a sinnsir a ré & a naimsir, & cia hairett ro battar i tticcernas a nduithce, i ndignit, no i nonoir diaidh i ndiaidh, & cred i an oidheadh fuairsiott.

an brathair bocht,
Michel O Clericch
10 Lughnasa 1636

*Do m'athair agus do mo mháthair,
a thug féith an léinn.*

Cethardai condagar du each elathain
.i. locc ₇ aimsior ocus persu ocus tuccait scribhind no fath aircc.

Félire Oengusso
c. 800 A.D.

PREFACE

Cill na Martra has been well served by other works, by individuals and groups such as the local Coiste Forbartha, which have dealt with its social and cultural history. This book therefore does not concentrate on those areas.

My thanks to the staff at the Boole Library, UCC; Trinity College Library, Dublin; National Archives, Dublin; Stella Cherry, Curator, and Dan Breen of Cork Public Museum and especially to Deirdre O'Carroll of Cork County Library.

Thanks also to the National Museum and Ordnance Survey Ireland for permission to reproduce items.

Thanks to Prof. Dáibhí Ó Cróinín of NUI Galway, whose comments on an earlier paper led to this book. Special thanks to Dr. John Crowley of UCC who kindly provided the Introduction.

Any opinions or errors are solely the author's.

INTRODUCTION

The story of settlement and the creation of place are of particular interest to the historian and the historical geographer. In compiling this rich history of Cill na Martra the author has added another significant layer to our understanding of a particular place. This is a story of a parish told literally from the ground up, beginning with the evolution of the landscape and the natural environment. It then proceeds to chart the history of the various peoples who have settled there from prehistoric times to the early twentieth century. The skills of the document-based historian are very much in evidence throughout this in-depth exploration of place. This book in the end breathes new life into a specific historical landscape and should be read by native and visitor alike.

Dr John Crowley,
Department of Geography,
University College Cork

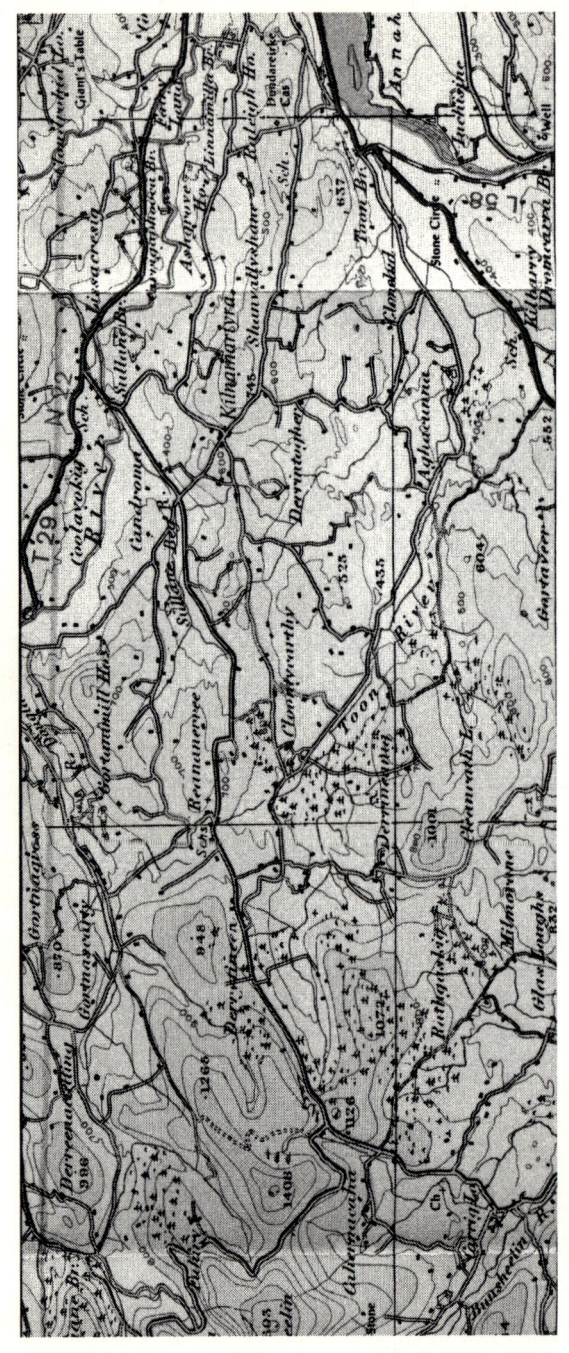

CHAPTER 1: PRE-HISTORY

History is, to a great extent, a function of geography, which in turn is a function—to some extent- of geology. It is fitting therefore to begin a history of Cill na Martra by locating the area geographically and briefly describing its geology.

'Cill na Martra is a small rural parish in West Cork,'[1] located c.30 miles west of Cork city. It appears on the Ordnance Survey 6-inch map on sheets 69 and 70. The dominant geological feature of the parish is a sandstone ridge running east-west through its centre, rising to 742 ft. (226 metres). This rock dates from the Devonian period 400 million years ago and is complemented by other such ridges to the north and south, the one on the northern side being named quite literally Comh-Drom (Codrum) , or perhaps more correctly Comhad-Drom[2], meaning 'companion ridge.' The central ridge extends for over nine miles from Sliabh Caoin (Sleaveen) near Macroom to Leac Mór in Renaniree on the western boundary of Cill na Martra.[3] This topography gives the district its more ancient name (but one which was still in use in living memory) of Tuath na Dromann, the Tribe(land) of the Ridges.

This landscape of east-west Old Red Sandstone (ORS) outcrops is typical of higher lands in Munster and 'reflects the fact that . . . the ORS . . . were folded along east-west axes, i.e., the whole lot was given a push from the south.'[4] This 'push' was during the Armorican Folding Period 250 million years ago. Also typical of this geological formation, the River Sullane and River Toon valleys run to the north and south respectively of the main ridge, in deep valleys descending to 250 ft. Dr. Kennan speaks of such a landscape being 'sculpted by fast-flowing, noisy torrents in deeply cut valleys...'[5] This geological fact finds its echo in the historical names of these rivers: An So-Lán (the easily flooded) and An Tonn (the [flood]wave).

Originally the river valleys would have been much deeper as the ridges of ORS were originally much higher, given the massive pressure of Plate Tectonics as continents collided to give this 'push' from the south. Indeed originally the 'mountain range formed in this way . . . was so high that it drew down the moisture from the prevailing south winds and made desert of the land in its lee. Today this ridge has been eroded down to stumps, surviving in Ireland as gentle hills of Old Red Sandstone, folding east to west through counties Waterford, Cork and Kerry.'[6]

We can already see, then, that the parish has an ancient landscape if we consider, for instance, that the Alps were formed a mere 20 million years ago.

It is not surprising, therefore, that the landscape also has evidence of human habitation from pre-historic times. We cannot say for certain when human beings first came to Ireland but the latest scholarship tells us the 'earliest evidence we have for human occupation in Ireland dates to about 8000 B.C., and for the next four thousand years people provided for themselves by fishing, hunting and gathering wild plants. However, changes began to take place from about 4000 B.C. onwards, with the gradual introduction of farming bringing domesticated cereals and animals from Britain and/or Northern France. Soon afterwards people began to build what we now call megalithic tombs . . . '[7]

The term 'megalithic' comes from the Greek *megas lithos*

2

meaning 'big stone,' and Cill na Martra has examples of these earliest remaining human constructs.

These include the stone alignment at Cools, which is unusual in that each of the two stones of the alignment seems to be aligned in a different direction; one clearly north-east to Mushera mountain; the other in a north-westerly direction to no discernible point now identifiable. The alignment of the former stone is typical. Prof. M.J. O'Kelly tells us there 'are two major concentrations of stone alignments, one in the north in Derry, Tyrone and Fermanagh, and the other in west Cork and Kerry . . . The Cork/Kerry alignments are consistently orientated NE-SW . . .'[8]

This orientation towards Mushera has a significance now lost but was probably religious. Dr. Daphne D.C. Pochin Mould notes that the 'concentration around Mushera in the Boggeragh Mountains is very striking. Mushera rises to 2,118 feet, has a well on the summit and is a landmark for many miles around . . . all this area was almost built over with stone circles, wedge-tombs, stone alignments, stone pairs and solitary standing stones.'[9]

Volume III of the Cork Archaeological Survey[10] (and the earlier Sites and Monuments record-SMR-completed in 1988) lists a large number of archaeological features in the parish. The following list includes the Archaeological Survey inventory number and classification for each site:

1. Megalithic Tombs
  6425 Renaniree
  6434 Rahoonagh East/West

2. Stone Circles
  6443 Gortanimill[11]
  6478 Renaniree
  6486 Rathoonagh East/West

3. **Radial Stone Cairn**
   6489 Gortnabinna

4. **Stone Rows and Standing Stone Pairs**
   6526 Renaniree
   6540 Candroma
   6546 Cools
   6575 Knocksaharn

5. **Single Standing Stone**
   6611 Ballyvoige
   6612 Ballyvoige
   6613 Ballyvoige
   6625 Caherdaha
   6626 Caherdaha
   6627 Candroma
   6652 Clohina
   6660 Coolavokig
   6661 Coolavokig
   6662 Coolavokig
   6663 Coolcaum
   6693 Derryfineen
   6694 Derryfineen
   6701 Dromreague
   6780 Knockroe
   6781 Knockroe
   6782 Knockroe
   6785 Knocksaharn
   6787 Kylefinchin
   6788 Kylefinchin
   6789 Kylefinchin
   6790 Lackmore

6791 Lackmore
6850 Prohus
6851 Rahoonagh East
6852 Raleigh South
6853 Raleigh South
6854 Raleigh South
6882 Aghacunna
6902 Caherdaha
6903 Candroma
6904 Candroma
6927 Dromreague
6967 Knockroe
6971 Knocksaharn

6. Fulachta Fiadh

7162 Candroma
7163 Candroma
7212 Cloontycarthy
7233 Coolavokig
7234 Coolavokig
7235 Coolavokig
7315 Derrintogher
7341 Dromreague
7342 Dromreague
7343 Dromreague
7344 Dromreague
7345 Dromreague
7346 Dromreague
7413 Gortanimill
7414 Gortanimill
7618 Knocksaharn
7735 Renaniree
7802 Candroma

7845 Renaniree

7. Cairns and Tumuli
7856 Coolavokig

8. Anomalous Stone Group
7923 Coolavokig

9. Ogham Stones
7991 Clohina   [no longer extant; possible inscription]

10. Ringforts
8069 Ballyvoige
8100 Brehaun
8114 Caherdaha
8115 Caherdaha
8119 Caherkereen
8177 Cloontycarthy
8178 Cloontycarthy
8191 Coolavokig
8192 Coolavokig
8193 Coolavokig
8248 Derrintogher
8266 Dromagarry
8328 Gortaneadin
8450 Kylefinchin
8451 Lackbeg
8452 Lackmore
8453 Lackmore
8466 Lisboy More
8547 Prohus
8548 Rath East
8570 Renaniree

8593 Shanballyshane
8658 Caherdaha
8674 Coolavokig

11. Cashels
8812 Dromreague
8833 Clohina

12. Souterrains (possible)
8996 Coolavokig
9022 Dromreague
9101 Rahoonagh East
9111 Shanballyshane

13. Enclosures
9177 Dromreague
9181 Rath West

14. Early Ecclesiastical Sites
9206 Kilmakaroge
9208 Clohina

15. Early Ecclesiastical Miscellanea
9216 Clohina (Bullaun Stone)
9229 Kilmakaroge (Bullaun Stone)
9235/36 (Bullaun Stones from Cill Lachtain in Clohina
 now in grounds of Renaniree church)
9243 Cross Slab from Clohina
 (now in Cork Public Museum according to the
 Archaeological Survey)[12]
9245 Possible 'Swastika' Cross Slab
 (was in the possession of local historian Conor
 Murphy in San Francisco at the end of the 19th

century; location now unknown)

16. **Holy Wells and Penitential Stations**
    9255 Ballyvoige (Tobar na bPian)
    9256 Ballyvoige (Tobar Lachtain)
    9262 Clohina
    9263 Clohina

17. **Horizontal-Wheeled Mills**
    9306 Cloontycarthy

18. **Burial Grounds and Burials**
    9316 Ballyvoige (cillín near Tobar na bPian)
    9323 Clohina
    9346 Kilmakaroge
    9799 Coolavokig (possible famine burial-ground)

19. **Tower Houses and Bawns**
    9476 Dundareirke

20. **Mass Rocks**
    9556 Candroma (no visible remains)

21. **Post Medieval**
    9635 Rahoonagh West (Clapper Bridge on Douglas River)
    9703 Caherkereen   (An Simné)

The area is obviously rich in archaeological remains.
As Seán Ua Súilleabháin writes:
'Ní hinniu ná inné a tháinig daoine ar dtúis chun an cheantair. Idir chúig mhíle bliain agus cheithre mhíle bliain ó shin is túisce leag daoine cos ar talamh ann go bhfuil aon rian fágtha acu ina ndiaidh, agus tuairisc dá réir againn orthu. B'iad so an

dream a thóg na 'tuamaí dinge' athá le feiscint . . . i Ré na nDoirí
. . . Idir dhá mhíle agus míle chúig céad bliain roim Chríost a mhair lucht na bhfulacht fiann, de réir dealraimh; táid siad ar Cluainte Cárthaigh, ar Cúil a' Bhuacaigh . . . agus i mbaill eile. Idir 1,500 agus 800 bliain roim Chríost a mhair na daoine a thóg na fáinní gallán . . . i Ré na nDoirí . . . Sa tarna leath den chéad mhíle bliain d'aois an Tiarna a tosnaíodh ar na liosanna a thógaint, agus feirmeóirí a chónaigh iontu . . . ' [13]

Some of the sites listed above are related. For example, the important early ecclesiastical site at Clohina (9208), which will be treated in more detail later, has the ancient burial ground (9323), possible ogham stone (7991), bullaun stones (9216, 9235,and 9236), cross slab (9243), possible cross slab (9245) and holy wells (9262, 9263) associated with it. Similarly, the stone circle (6478) at Renaniree is contiguous to a stone row (6526) and fulacht fiadh (7845). In the first example at Clohina we can see that each individual archaeological feature forms part of a single unit; in the second at Renaniree we cannot be sure whether each site stands alone or was viewed by its makers as connected to the contiguous sites.

It should also be noted that the above listing of sites, while impressive, is not exhaustive. Only one mass rock site, itself no longer extant, is listed. Local tradition, however, identifies such sites at Shanballyshane and Knocksaharn, where the name Carraig a'tSagairt still attests. There was also a mass rock in Caherkereen, in use until the 19th century, and another at Aghacunna. The place-names Móinteán an Aifrinn and Móinéar an Aifrinn in the Douglas River valley north of Renaniree also attest to mass being said at those sites in Penal times.

There were also many unrecorded and now destroyed sites. One such site was uncovered in a farmyard in Knockroe in the 1970s during building work. This was not marked on any map or remembered in folklore but was clearly a fulacht fiadh, being composed of a shallow pit covered in dark, burnt material. Neither is the souterrain in the lios at Caherdaha listed. Further examples of features not listed could also be given.

Local Postman Peter Murphy
at an archaelogical site in Knockroe

The horizontal mill found at Cloontycarthy was discovered during drainage works in 1981 and was subsequently excavated by archaeologists from UCC. The surviving timbers are now on display in Cork Public Museum. Dendrochronological analysis of the timbers gave a date of c.833 A.D. The excavation showed the surviving penstock was over 2 metres long and was water-driven. The mill incorporated a rectangular wheelhouse roughly four metres square in size, within which were found the remains of a horizontal waterwheel hub and eight dished paddles. A large fragment of a millstone was found nearby where the mill tailrace would have been.

The date derived from the timbers fits in well with general archaeological knowledge of Irish horizontal mills. Colin Rynne (who did the excavation at Cloontycarthy) has written that 'of the

27 Irish watermill sites dated to the period 630–1228, just over half (56%) were built with timbers felled in the period 770–850.'[14] He has also shown that the earliest Irish documentary evidence for the horizontal-wheeled mill is to be found in the *De Ceithri Slichtaib Athgábala*, a late 6th or early 7th century law tract.[15] It is thought that the horizontal watermill was first invented in Greece in the 1st century B.C. Given that examples have been found in Ireland (including one found at Mashanaglass some few miles to the east of Cloontycarthy, near Macroom), the Hebrides and Scandinavia, but none in England, it was postulated that it may have been introduced into Ireland by the Vikings. In the Hebrides such mills are still referred to as 'Norse mills.' However, recent scholarship has shown this technology was in use in Ireland long before the coming of the Vikings and it is now thought the technology flowed in the opposite direction; that is to say from Ireland to the Hebrides, which were of course then part of the Gaelic world.[16]

Cloontycarthy Horizontal Mill

Thus the Cloontycarthy site shows Cill na Martra was at the

cutting edge of technology in early medieval times. Indeed it might be argued this site ranks as one of the historically most important in the parish.

Tradition also recalls another episode from the dawn of history in the parish. The topography, as already outlined, would suggest that the ridge-tops would be the natural arteries of communication, especially as the valleys would have been heavily wooded before the activity of humans eventually altered the landscape. Vestiges of this aboriginal woodland still remain on either side of the main ridge; Prohus wood lying to the north and the Gearagh to the south—both of which are classified by Cork County Council as Proposed National Heritage Areas. Local folklore records an ancient highway running through the parish, along the main ridge.

The Bealach Feabhradh (Way of the Hillbrow), sometimes written Bealach Abhra, ran from Sleaveen (Sliabh Caoin) on the edge of what is now Macroom town—where Brian Ború's battle with Maolmhuadh, killer of Brian's brother Mathghamhain, ended with Maolmhuadh's death. It was an important route in ancient times, possibly being the local section of a great Munster highway of the same name which ran through north Cork and on to what is now Co. Limerick. The Ballyhoura Hills still carry the name. We also read in Seathrún Céitinn's *Foras Feasa ar Éirinn* an account of the laying out of the bounds of the diocese of Limerick at the synod of Rathbrassil in 1100 giving 'Bealach Feabhradh is Tulach Léis' (Tullylease) as being part of the southern reaches of the diocese. In Cill na Martra a few galláns or standing stones are still to be found, more or less in a straight line, along the main ridge, perhaps marking this ancient highway. As Paul Mulligan noted, some standing stones 'may have acted as boundary markers or route indicators.' [17] The modern roadway still follows the line of the ridge-top on to Cill na Martra village.

The Bealach Feabhradh continued westward through the site

of the modern village on to Cathair Deaghaidh, where it turned north to cross the Sullane Beag at Áth an Tiompáin. It continued on to Ballyvourney to meet the other ancient highway from Kerry, Bealach Mogh Ruith, at Lománach. The modern roadway still more or less follows this line, with the bridge over the river at Candroma being only yards from the original Áth an Tiompáin. Some would interpret the word 'tiompán' here as 'drum,' from the Latin 'tympanum.' Indeed this is the meaning given in Dineen. Conor Murphy derives the meaning from a standing stone which is bulky but not high.[18] That this derivation is correct is shown by the Scots Gaelic Clach na Tiompàn, a partially destroyed four stone ring in Pertshire whose remaining stones fit this description.[19] Más an Tiompáin on the side of Mount Brandon also carries the name.

Bealach Mogh Ruith was named after a famous druid who was a native of Valentia island. The name signifies 'Follower of the Wheel,' i.e. a devotee of the sun-god. According to the ancient tale *Forbhais Droma Dámhgháire* (which has been called the Táin of Munster) he was called on to save the army of Munster during a battle near present day Knocklong, Co. Limerick. The tale is recounted in the manuscript known as *The Book of Lismore* and is also mentioned in *The Book of Leinster* thereby showing 'that the tale was known in the twelfth century or earlier.'[20]

The *Forbhais* tells of Cormac Mac Airt invading from Leinster and using magic against the army of Munster. In desperation, Fiacha Muilleathan, king of Munster, sends for Mogh Ruith. Tradition tells of the druid coming along the ancient highway named after him in a chariot pulled by wild oxen. Modern archaeology shows that the Irish horse in these early times was a small animal and oxen were used as draught animals. The manuscript source agrees with the tradition, naming the oxen as Luath Tréan and Luath Lis from Sliabh Mis in Kerry.

Just as the Bealach Mogh Ruith runs by the early ecclesiastical site associated with St. Gobnait in Ballyvourney, the Bealach Feabhradh runs by some of the most significant ancient sites in Cill na Martra. As already mentioned, the ancient highway turns north at Cathair Deaghaidh. There are two ringforts on the hillside here, with a third not far away. This site takes its name from the Clann Deaghaidh, who feature prominently in ancient tales. As Conor Murphy puts it: 'this ancient warrior clan took its name from Deaghaidh, son of Sen, son of Oilioll Earann . . .'[21] Deaghaidh and his followers were expelled from their native Ulster by the Clann Rudhraighe some time before the Christian era. Cúroí Mac Dáire of Cathair Conroí in Kerry, who appears in the Craobh Rua tales of Ulster, is perhaps the most famous of this clan. The Ulster origins of his tribe explains why somebody from Munster appears in the Ulster Cycle tales with Cuchulainn—a fact which has puzzled some writers. It is also worth noting that in the *Forbhais,* Mogh Ruith chose as his reward for defeating the Leinstermen the territory of the Fir Muighe (Fermoy), where today can be found Carn Tighearnaigh Mhic Deaghaidh, the tumulus at the summit of Corrin Hill. Might it be speculated that Mogh Ruith was of the Clann Deaghaidh himself (this clan also had Kerry connections around modern day Castleisland) and travelled along the highway named for him as far as his kinsmen at Cathair Deaghaidh, where he joined the Bealach Feabhradh which he followed to the battle site in Co. Limerick and that others of the clan, such as the Tighearnach buried on Corrin Hill, got land from him in the Fermoy area? The tale itself is of course pseudo-historical but may contain some grains of historical truth as many myths do.

Possible Royal Inauguration Site

As the debate about the proposed road through the Tara-Skryne valley shows, it is now recognised by scholars that landscapes need to be viewed in an integrated, holistic way to gain an understanding of individual sites and artifacts contained within them. As we have seen, the Bealach Feabhradh running along the main ridge passes by a number of archaeological sites. Many of these have been commented on in isolation by various works over the years. However, an examination of a few almost contiguous sites, including crucially one hitherto almost unrecorded site, gives an interpretation previously unrecognised.

The *chanson de geste,* dating from the Norman invasion, describes the contemporary political scene in Ireland during the late 12th century: 'En yrland erent reis plusur . . . '[In Ireland there were many kings]. We can safely say kings had been even more numerous in earlier eras. Francis J. Byrne estimates: 'In fact, there were probably no less than 150 kings in the country at any given date between the fifth and twelfth centuries. Since the total population was probably well under half a million, this multiplicity of royalty is all the more remarkable.' [22] Each king ruled over his own tribal kingdom or *tuath.* Tuath na Dromann, therefore, can safely be assumed to have had its own king from earliest times.

This development of local kingship among early peoples has been traced to the Bronze Age: 'While the early farming societies of the Neolithic Age had been relatively egalitarian . . . Bronze Age societies developed dominant social elites.' [23] Anthropologists know this kind of hierarchical society as a 'chiefdom,' and it was typical of the organisation of Celtic societies across Europe.[24] Not having been disrupted by Roman imperialism, this kind of social organisation survived in Ireland and Gaelic Scotland until Early Christian times and even into much later eras and did not finally disappear until the collapse of the Gaelic polity in Ireland in the 17th century and the Scottish Highlands in the 18th century.

As Heywood writes: 'Early Christian Ireland was a complex mosaic of hundreds of local kingdoms and dozens of over-kingdoms. An ordinary king (*rí tuaithe*) was the ruler of a *tuath,* . . . the territory of a *tuath* could be very small, often less than a hundred square miles (160 square kilometres). Each *tuath* would have its capital, usually a small ringfort or crannog; a church or monastery; and an inauguration site . . . '[25]

With the rise of the Uí Néill and the contention between them and Brian Ború of the Dál gCais to be *Árd Rí* the political consolidation led to a loss of status by the smaller *ríthe tuaithe*. 'The title *rí tuaithe* went out of use and was replaced by *taoiseach*, meaning chief . . . '[26] This passing of the old order has tended to be attributed to consolidation in the face of Viking incursions. Máire Herbert maintains, however, that 'it would seem that the Viking presence did not so much overturn the past as accelerate changes already in train, especially in the nature of royal power. The greater Irish provincial kingships had already strengthened at the expense of smaller political units during the 8th century, and around the mid 9th century, in the wake of the establishment of Viking settlements, Ireland's premier dynasty, the Uí Néill, actively began to shape a coalition of the country's major kingdoms . . . '[27]

Therefore the ancient territory of Tuath na Dromann would have had a local *rí tuaithe* from earliest times down, possibly to the 8th century.

Dáibhí Ó Cróinín asks regarding the residences of such kings: 'But what were these houses fit for kings?'[28] Drawing on written sources and details of archaeological excavation, he concludes that *ríthe tuaithe* did not live in palaces or houses noticeably larger than those of the *mruigfer* (strong farmers) as described in the ancient text *Crith Gablach*. He quotes the archaeologist Chris Lynn who 'pointed out that the mention in the laws of cartloads of wattles or loads of rushes as appropriate fines for damaging parts of a king's house supports his view that the houses built for kings were little different from those of the lower grades of society. The only obvious contrast might have been in the number of houses on the site or in the occasional construction of an outer wall or revetment around the outer bank of the rath, giving the mound an impressive appearance . . . '[29] Byrne also refers to the 8th century law tract *Crith Gablach* which describes the king's *dún* thus: 'What is the proper fortress for a king who is in constant residence at the head of his *tuath*? Seven score feet of full measure the size of his fortress in every direction. Seven feet [the width of] its ditch; twelve feet its depth. It is then that he is king when ramparts of base clientship surround him.' [30]

As Byrne remarks, the size of the ramparts 'was visible expression of the number of base clients who had built it.' [31] The importance of a king was in direct proportion to the amount of clients he had; the whole polity being organised in a complex series of *frithfolaid* or mutual obligations as shown by the various early law tracts and the later *Lebor na gCeart*.

All of this shows that the 'king's house is not normally of such grandeur as to distinguish it from those of ordinary mortals.' [32] The only distinguishing feature would be a more impressive set of outer ramparts. In the case of a minor *rí tuaithe* it is reasonable to assume that the residence would be an ordinary lios or rath but one which was multi-vallate rather than uni-vallate as would have been the norm.

There is just such a lios in the townland of Kylefinchin. To the modern observer it appears uni-vallate, as it did when described in the *Southern Star* over 30 years ago by C.J.F. McCarthy as 'a fine embanked earthwork at an altitude of 627 feet commanding a very good view of the parish.' [33] However, Conor Murphy writing in 1898 described it as 'a very large fort with a double embankment encircling it.' [34] This description of Kylefinchin lios fits the description of the residence of a *rí tuaithe*. This can be further confirmed by comparison with Garranes ringfort, some 25 miles or so to the east, generally accepted as definitely a royal site and possibly synonymous with Rath Raithleann of the Eoghanachta Raithlinn. Like Kylefinchin it is at an elevation of c.600 feet. Seán P. Ó Riordáin, who excavated Garranes, tells us the 'building and occupation of ring-forts extended over a very long period, at least from the Early Iron age, throughout the Early Christian period, and persisted into late Medieval times.'[35] Ó Riordáin dated Garranes to the 5th century and Kylefinchin is probably of the same era, though we cannot be sure without excavation. Garranes has three concentric banks, an overall diameter of 360 feet, with the inner enclosure measuring 220 feet across.[36] The inner enclosure of Kylefinchin (north to south) is about 285 feet.

Inaguration Stone

A necessary appendage to a Gaelic royal site was an inauguration site. This need not necessarily be contiguous to the residential site, as shown by the Uí Néill inauguration site at Tullahogue and the Dál gCais site at Mágh Adhair. However, for a small *tuath* one might expect the inauguration site and the residential site to be reasonably close. A common motif, though not a universal one, to help recognise an inauguration site is the presence of an inauguration stone. Francis J. Byrne quotes a 17th century narrative from Gaelic Scotland describing the inauguration of the Lord of the Isles: 'There was a square stone, seven or eight feet long, upon which he stood, denoting that he should walk in the footsteps and uprightness of his predecessors . . . '[37] The *Lia Fáil,* Stone of Scone and inauguration stone at Tullahogue, destroyed by Mountjoy after Kinsale, confirm the theme. Haywood tells us the Lordship of the Isles 'was a self-consciously Irish orientated polity . . . The inauguration ceremony of the Lords was reminiscent- deliberately so- of that of the ancient Scottish kings of Dal Riata as it involved the use of a square stone on which was carved the shape of a man's footprint. The new Lord was expected to place his foot in the print as a sign that he would walk in the footprints and uprightness of his predecessors.' [38] The inauguration stone of Ruairí Ua Conchubhair, last High-King of Ireland, is now preserved at Clonallis House, home of the O'Connor Don, lineal descendant. This stone also has a footprint carved on it.

Inaguration Stone

A similar stone is to be found in a field less than half a mile west of Kylefinchin lios. This is a singleton large boulder, roughly two and a half feet high. It has the imprint of a human foot carved into it, with a second less perfect imprint alongside the first. The imprint is obviously man-made and not a natural feature; the carved indent even matches the arch of the human foot perfectly. The size of the foot is smaller than the average modern foot, being roughly a size six, reflecting presumably the smaller stature of people some 15 or so centuries ago.

This archaeological feature seems to be almost unknown to the literature. It is not noted by the Ordnance Survey or by the Archaeological Inventory of Co. Cork. Neither is there any surviving local folklore about it. The only reference to it is found in the National Schools' folklore project where Neans Ní Shúilleabháin collected in 1938 a story that a Penal era priest offering prayers over a coffin at Lúibín na gCorp was surprised by soldiers and to escape 'do léim sé ón mbóthar agus chuaidh leis an léim sin ceathamhradh míle taobh thuaidh den bhóthar agus an áit gur tháinig sé anuas ná ar chloch agus tá rian a bhróige chlé agus leath dá bhróig dheis ar an gcloic shin fós.' The story finishes with a warning that bad luck falls on anyone who puts his foot into the imprint on the rock.

The third element of a Gaelic royal inauguration site was religious. St. Lachtain's site at Clohina, which will be treated in greater detail later, fulfills this element.

The most recent scholar to write on this subject, Elizabeth FitzPatrick, holds that finding 'inauguration sites of the Gaelic lordships on the landscape is a difficult task' and in particular the 'venues of the Munster Gaelic lordships . . . have remained elusive.' She recommends using archaeological reasoning and other techniques to identify such sites. As we have seen above, this type of approach suggests strongly that this site was the inauguration site of Tuath na Dromann.

Notes and References

[1] *Cill na Martra: Muscraí, Co. Chorcaí*, Coiste Forbartha, 1995, p.1.
[2] '..Comhad-drom láimh le Mochromtha...', Cobhar, 'Maoilsheachlainn Ó Dubhgáin' in *An Músgraigheach*, 2, Fóghmhar, 1943, p.4.
[3] Barry O'Brien, *Macroom, A Chronicle*, No.1, 1990, p.23
[4] Pádhraig S. Kennan, *Written in Stone*, 1995, p.31
[5] Kennan, *op. cit.*, p.29

[6] Michael Viney, *Ireland: A Smithsonian Natural History*, 2003, p.18
[7] Elizabeth Shee Twohig, *Irish Megalithic Tombs*, 2004, p.7
[8] Michael J. O'Kelly, *Early Ireland: An Introduction to Irish Prehistory*, 1989, pp.230-1
[9] Daphne D.C. Pochin Mould, *Discovering Cork*, 1991, p.22
[10] Power *et al.*, *Archaeological Inventory of County Cork*, Vol. 3, 1997
[11] Megalithic scholar Aubrey Burl theorises this is orientated towards the mid-winter sunset; the opposite of Newgrange. Cf. Burl, *A Guide to the Stone Circles of Britain, Ireland and Brittany*, 1995, p.220
[12] This stone is not now in the Museum
[13] Seán Ua Súilleabháin, 'Baile Mhúirne, Cill na Martra agus Cluain Droichead Múscraí', p.661
[14] Colin Rynne, 'Horizontal Mills in Mediaeval Ireland', 1998-99, p.251
[15] *ibid.*
[16] See www.culturehebrides.com
[17] Paul Mulligan, *A Short Guide to Irish Antiquities*, 2005, p.63
[18] Conor Murphy, 'Parish of Cill-na-Martra; Its Ancient Topography and Traditions, Part II',1898, footnote p.19
[19] A description and image of this ring can be accessed at www.megalithic.co.uk
[20] Seán Ó Duinn (trans.), *Forbhais Droma Dámhgháire: The Siege of Knocklong*, 1992, p.5
[21] Conor Murphy, *op. cit.*, p.12
[22] Francis J. Byrne, *Irish Kings and High Kings*, 2001 (2nd ed.), p.7
[23] John Haywood, *The Celts: Bronze Age to New Age*, 2004, p.11
[24] *ibid.*, p.12
[25] *ibid.*, p.130
[26] *ibid.*
[27] Máire Herbert, 'Ireland and Scotland: the Foundations of a Relationship', 2000, pp.19-27
[28] Dáibhí Ó Cróinín, *Early Medieval Ireland 400-1200*, 1995, p.73
[29] *ibid.*, pp.74-5
[30] Quoted in F.J. Byrne, *op. cit.*, p.32
[31] *ibid.*
[32] Ó Cróinín, *op. cit.*, p.71
[33] *Southern Star* 15 August 1970
[34] Conor Murphy, *op. cit.*, pp.1-19
[35] Seán P. Ó Riordáin, *Antiquities of the Irish Countryside*, 1979, p.31
[36] J.C. Coleman, *Journeys into Muskerry*, n.d., p.61
[37] F.J. Byrne, *op. cit.*, p.20
[38] *ibid.*, pp.124-125

CHAPTER 2: PLACES AND NAMES

The Parish

In seeking to give an account of the history of Cill na Martra it is necessary to define what is meant by the phrase 'parish of Cill na Martra'. To anyone living in or familiar with the locality this may appear strange, however the familiar is often the most strange. People living there will generally understand the phrase to refer to the (Catholic) religious parish of Cill na Martra (or Kilnamartyra), comprising the following townlands (with their acreage given in brackets):

Aghacunna	(401)
Ballyvoige	(587) [Ballyvoge on OS map]
Brehaun	(212)
Caherkereen	(386)
Caherdaha	(218)
Candroma	(459)
Coolavokig	(923)
Cools	(126)
Coolcaum	(260)
Clonclud	(273)
Clohina	(648) [Cloheena on OS]
Cloontycarthy	(541)
Derrintogher	(186)
Dromreague	(436)
Dromagarry	(221)

Dromonig	(306)
Dundareirke	(310)
Derryfineen	(480)
Derragh	(439)
Derreenacartan	(102)
English Garden	(22)
Gortaneadin	(192)
Gortanimill	(593)
Gortnabinna	(780)
Inchinahoury	(159)
Knockroe	(453)
Kylefinchin	(203)
Knocksaharn	(447)
Kilmakaroge	(228)
Leac Beg	(307) [Lack on OS]
Leac More	(224)
Lisboy Beg	(440)
Lisboy More	(533)
Prohus	(278)
Parnanillane	(155)
Rahoonagh East	(331)
Rahoonagh West	(367)
Renaniree	(469) [Reananeree on OS]
Rath East	(344)
Rath West	(259)
Shanballyshane	(235) [Shanvallyshane on OS]

However, the official or civil parish of Kilnamartery (as it is spelled by the Ordnance Survey) is somewhat different. The townlands of

Curraheen	(70)
Glebe	(40)

Inchibrackane   (95)
Raleigh North   (267)
Raleigh South   (340)

are added to the parish; while Candroma, Dromagarry, Dromonig, English Garden, Inchinahoury and Prohus are lost to Clondrohid civil parish and Coolavokig, Rathoonagh East and West and Rath East and West are in Ballyvourney civil parish.

To add another dash of confusion, while any local person would consider all the townlands ceded to other civil parishes to be part of Cill na Martra, he or she would also consider the Glebe and Raleigh South as being part of the parish, but not Curraheen, Inchibrackane or Raleigh North.

This confusion regarding parish boundaries, between civil and religious parishes, is a national rather than a local phenomenon and stems from the re-organisation of the Catholic parish structure in the post-Penal and post-Famine era when the vastly changed legal, social and demographic situation necessitated a reform of ecclesiastical administrative structure that had pertained from medieval or even earlier times. As one writer put it almost a century ago: 'owing to a variety of causes, but especially the exigencies of population and income, wholesale changes have been made in the extent and boundaries of parishes within the past two centuries and a half. This is particularly true of the Catholic division in which, frequently if not as a rule, the parishes have lost not only their original bounds and entity but even their ancient names.'[1] A more modern scholar of medieval record sources agrees: 'the medieval parish divisions correspond to a great extent to later civil parishes …Anyone interested in tracing the history of a modern Catholic parish back to the middle ages will need therefore to establish the relationship between the catholic and civil parishes.'[2]

This fluidity of overlapping local identities is something which perhaps should have attracted the attention of scholars, from historians to sociologists and political scientists, as it has an influence on the way people think and act even today.

It has been claimed that the modern parishes of Cill na Martra and Ballyvourney, along with part of Clondrohid, were one parish, known by the ancient name of Tuath na Dromann, until 1858 when they became separate parishes. As Ua Súilleabháin puts it: 'Aon pharóiste amháin ab ea Baile Mhúirne agus Cill na Martra, b'fhéidir ó lár na hochtú haoise déag go dtí an bhliain 1858. Tá an méid sin soiléir ach liosta na sagart paróiste i nDeoiseas Chluana a scrudú'.[3]

Given that each parish has different patron saints it is unlikely they were one parish in very ancient times. The origin of the parish structure in Ireland is generally considered by modern scholars to be a Norman initiative. 'Parishes as territorial units were essentially an Anglo-Norman innovation and the decree of the Synod of Cashel in 1172 ordering the payment of tithes probably marks the beginning of parochial organisation in Ireland.'[4] The organisation of the pre-Norman church into *paruchiae* is a matter of considerable debate among scholars, with sharply differing views being proposed.

It is, therefore, likely that the two parishes were amalgamated in relatively modern times in historical terms. This is also the accepted version in the official history of the Diocese of Cloyne issued to mark the Millennium, where we read: 'with the relaxation of the penal Laws, Baile Bhúirne and Cill na Martra became one parish. The parishes were separated in 1858.'[5]

This view is also in keeping with the historical fact that parishes of ancient times were much smaller and therefore more plentiful than in modern times. The Diocese of Cloyne, for example, currently has 46 parishes, including Cill na Martra. When John de Swafham was bishop of Cloyne, between 1363 and 1367 he assembled all available diocesan documents and had them copied on to parchment. These parchments were then sewn together, the bottom of one on to the top of the next. Other documents were added at later times until eventually it formed a long roll measuring 17 feet in length and covered events from 1227 to 1423. It became known as the Pipe Roll of Cloyne. We can see from it that many modern parishes, both civil and religious, are made up of a number of smaller ancient parishes. The parish of Ballyhea, to take one example, includes some or all of the older parishes of Ardskeagh, Coolene, Impric, Aglishdrinagh and Shandrum; and contains the ruins of five churches dating from ancient times.

As regards Tuath na Dromann, it may be that it was the pattern of landholding under the MacCarthy lordship of medieval times (of which we shall treat in greater detail later) which led to the union; and it is under MacCarthy auspices that Cill na Martra appears in the Pipe Roll of Cloyne: 'Item, idem Dermicius tenet in Dromyn...'[6] Dromyn here is Tuath na Dromann. The Pipe Roll tells us that Diarmuid Mór MacCárthaigh 'holds five townlands and one thousand acres of wood, at the lord's will, by the service of homage, fealty and common suit, and 40s yearly.'[7]

Local Placenames [8]

'The local place names of Cill na Martra have come down to us in an excellent state of preservation, which is appreciable from the fact that not a few of them are of pagan origin, and in their course down through countless centuries have suffered comparatively little by corruption ...This must be attributed to the fact that the native language always continued in use ...'[9] Conor Murphy continues by saying that these local placenames 'take us back several centuries, or beyond the reach of any documentary records now in existence.'[10]

Cill na Martra (the church of the relics), Kilnamartyra: the word 'relics' here means the remains of the dead. The relics in question were those of St. Lachtain, whose reliquary shrine, Lámh Lachtaín, is still extant, though the relics it contained (presumably his hand and arm bones) are now lost. Cill na Martra traces its origin to the founding by this local saint of his Cill at Clohina in the 6th century. Following his death, recorded in the Annals in 622 AD, his relics became a source of pilgrimage for people seeking cures for ailments, hence the name Cill na Martra.

Dún Dá Radharc (stronghold/fortress of two views), Dundareirke: This name refers to the view from the central ridge into the valleys on either side. Here the Uí Fhloinn had their Dún and the MacCarthys later erected a castle or tower house, a portion of which still remains. Some authorities, including Don Philip O'Sullivan Beare, have given it as Dún Deagh Radharc – the fort of the good view. However, the invariable local pronunciation of the middle element as 'Dá' is borne out by the 17th century poem from the neighbouring parish of Ballyvourney ('amharc' being synonymous with 'radharc'):

'Fíor cháidh saor fhlaithe
   Feardha-choin ná géilfeadh;
A d-tuath threibh Uí Fhloinn
   Fearann dhruim na féile

Póir, d'fhuil chlann Ithe
   Sliocht Chonaire, ró éachd gliath,
' Na n-Dún-Bhrúgh dá-amharc;
   Comh throm mhuil a tSlé' chaoin.'

As further proof it can also be mentioned that noted scholar Fr. Paul Walsh in a 1923 review of Prof. Charles Plummer's edition of *Bethada Naém nÉrenn* quoted the 19th century Gaelic scribe Mícheál Óg Ó Longáin as giving Dún Dá Radharc as the true form of the name.[11]

It is to be regretted that the official publication An tOrdú

Logainmneacha (Ceantair Gaeltachta) 2004 gives Dún Dea Radharc in error; not, unfortunately, the only error therein.

Doire Each (oak grove of the horses), Derragh: Darach- a place abounding in oak trees is sometimes given as the name. This does not fit with local pronunciation. Here is found Carraig na Mactíre (wolf rock); this district around Renaniree is (one of the many nationally) where the last wolf in Ireland is reputed to have been killed towards the end of the 18th century. At any rate the name suggests the area was home to wolves in previous centuries.

Gort na Binne (field of the peak), Gortnabinna.

Leac (flagstone or standing stone) Lack: Leac More and Beg townlands each contain a standing stone.

Doire Finghín (Finghín's oak grove) Derryfineen: the name Finghín, popular among the MacCarthys from an early date, is still used in the district; usually anglicised as Florence or Florry.

Cluainte an Chárthaigh (MacCarthy's dells or meadows), Cloontycarthy: here is found Páirc an Teampaill (church field) which suggests an early ecclesiastical site. The Civil Survey refers to it as Cloontikeartin which suggests an alternative name of Cluainte Ceártan – meadows of the forge or place of iron smelting.

Rath (ringfort), Rath East/West: the rath or ringfort is still extant. An older name for the area is Doire an Choirpe (oak grove of the rock ledge). A 19th century poet from here was known as Amhlaoibh a' Chuirpe [Ó Loingsigh]. Murphy gives a variant meaning to 'Cuirpe' as 'mischievous wickedness'. Both meanings are attested in Dineen. The topographical meaning is the more likely as 'coirpe' in Murphy's sense is an adjective rather than a noun, as in the formula 'Doire an Choirpe' (the 'o' and 'u' are interchangeable in the spelling, as for example in 'oifig an phuist/phoist'). Besides, the eponymous Amhlaoibh is hardly likely to have revelled in the 'wicked' epithet.

Gort an Imill (field of the boundary or edge), Gortanimill: this is the generally accepted meaning. However, an alternative derivation is from Gort Áth' na Míleadh (the field at the ford of the warriors). At least one older native of the parish always pronounced the name as 'gort-a-na-meel', which suggests the latter derivation. An Inquisition (12th of James I) following the death of a rebel Dermitius MacDowell Oge Carty in 1601 gives the name as 'Gortnimeale', which also supports this meaning. The ford referred to is nearby on the Douglas River and is named Áth an Bhuaidh (the ford of victory). Local tradition has a tale of an ancient battle spread over two days. On the first day an invading group from the east was victorious over local warriors at Lúibín na gCorp, by the side of Bealach Feabhradh on the eastern side of the parish. On the following day the local fighters had regrouped on the western boundary and battle was again joined. Here the invaders were annihilated. A short distance from the ford, on the Ballyvourney side of the river, is Cathair Ceárnadh (stone fort of victory). This encounter was described in an ancient manuscript now unfortunately lost. In an appendix to his *Lectures on the Manuscript Materials of Ancient Irish History* the great Gaelic scholar Eugene O'Curry lists Argain Dune Dubglaise or the Slaughter of Dun Dubhglaise among the lost historic tales mentioned in *The Book of Leinster*. In a footnote he says this tale is unknown to him.[12] Murphy notes that the 19th century poet Peadar Sheághain [O'Connor], a native of the parish who moved to Bantry, said the Cathair was originally known as Cathair Átha Cearnaigh. The nearby townland of Gort na Fuinnsean in Ballyvourney parish has the remains of a mound called Leaba a' Bhuaidh – perhaps the burial place of local heroes killed in the fight.

Cloch Adhnadh (the fire-kindling stone), Clohina: here was located Cill Lachtain. The origin of the name probably lies in pre-Christian times. The stone itself is 20ft. high, 18 in breadth and some eight ft. thick. Its name suggests pagan origins. The fact that Cill Lachtain was located here conforms to the general tendency in early Irish history where the new faith simply Christianised existing important pagan sites.

Réidh na nDoirí (the rough land of the oak groves), Renaniree.

Gort an Éadain (field of the hill-brow), Gortaneadin: Éadan is a very popular term in Gaelic toponomy. Art Ó Maolfabhail interprets Éadan in placenames as referring to the brow of the face (i.e. a body part) and says: 'Tá an focal seo ina mhír thosaigh i mbreis agus céad baile fearainn …'[13] The topographical meaning is the more likely; compare Dún Éadain (Edinburgh) where the castle sits on a large volcanic rock.

Cill Mágh Cearóg (church of the plain of the young stag), Kilmakaroge: there is an ancient Cill still extant but nothing is known concerning it. As early foundations are usually associated with a particular saint, whose name is often given in hypocoristic form, it might be posited that the root name is Cill Mo-Chearbhóg. O'Donoghue gives Cill Maciarog, whose feast he gives as 7 May. But as O'Hanlon states this saint is associated with an area in what is now Co. Tyrone, we can discount this.[14] It could also refer to 'Cill Mo-Chiaróg', the hypocoristic form of some local saint named Ciar (dark-haired) who was forgotten even in ancient days. As the *Archaeological Inventory of County*

Cork states: 'Townland name, bullaun stone and size of enclosure suggest possible early ecclesiastical site.'[15] Recent research may suggest another possibility. Colmán Etchingham has written of recent studies which show 'the persistence up to about 700 AD of burial other than in consecrated Christian cemeteries. Archaeologically, this practice manifests itself as isolated burials, circular enclosures and kindred/familial cemeteries.'[16] Perhaps the enclosure at Kilmakaroge may have been such an ancient burial place which continued into the Christian era but was subsequently sanitised by ascribing 'Cill' to it. The fact that such 'Cills' continued in use to the modern era for the burial of unbaptised children may show a remarkable historical continuity of over a millennium.

Doirín na Ceártan (little oak grove of the forge), Derreenacartan: O'Donoghue theorises a connection with iron smelting.

Lios Buí (yellow lios), Lisboy More/Beg: a ringfort is still extant. Alternatively, it could derive from Lios Baoi, after the druidess Baoi, wife of Dinioch, the famous druid of the Múscraidhe. Oileán Baoi and Cuan Baoi (Dursey Is. and Bantry Bay) also hold the name. Baoi and Dinioch are mentioned in the oldest surviving book of Irish legends and tales, *Leabhar na hUidhre* (known in English as the Book of the Dun Cow). It was compiled between 1090 and 1106 but is based on much earlier sources now lost. It has been described as the earliest exclusively Gaelic document in existence and the oldest surviving record of Irish literature.[17]

Achadh an Chonnaigh (field of the firewood), Aghacunna.

Cluain Clud (dell or sheltered meadow of the mud), Cloncud.

Cúil Cam (narrow or crooked recess or corner), Coolcaum.

Cnoc Rua (red hill), Knockroe: as Conor Murphy points out, 'rua' is not a bright red but brownish-red. In the 1960s the descendants of a family from Knockroe who had emigrated to Australia at the start of the 20th century visited Cill na Martra to see where the family originated. The emigrants had bought a farm in Australia which they named 'Brown Hill'.

Baile Uí Bhuaigh (place of the Ó Buaigh), Ballyvoige: incorrectly given as 'Ballyvoge' by the Ordnance Survey. In a manuscript by one of the Four Masters, Mícheál Ó Cléirigh, now in the Royal Irish Academy there is a listing of pre-Norman kings among whom is recorded Ó Lodaigh, taoiseach of Tuaithe na Druma.[18] It has been suggested that this is a scribal error for Ó Bodaigh and hence Ó Buaigh. A land deed sworn on the 20 October 1714 recording the sale by David and Mary Donnellan 'of Macrompe' of these lands to Henry Baldwin gives the name as 'Ballywigg', a pronunciation which was still in use by some in modern times.

Doire an Tóchair (oak grove of the causeway), Derrintogher.

Cnoc Satharainn (the hill of Satharann), Knocksaharn: Murphy interprets this as the pagan deity Saturn, who was venerated for introducing agriculture and other useful arts. O'Donoghue posits 'Sabhrainn' as the root. Placenames scholar Canon John Lyons guesses that 'Sabhrann, the ancient name of the Lee, seems to be preserved in Knocksaharn, in the parish of Kilnamartera, although it is three or four miles distant from the river.'[19] Anyone familiar with local pronunciation will know that O'Donoghue and Lyons cannot be correct. Neither does proper pronunciation admit 'Saturday's Hill'. O'Donoghue also incorrectly posits

'Cnoc Sorachain'.

Na Cúla (the hill-backs), Cools: given that we have the plural here we can be sure of not falling prey to the common error of 'the confusion between these two elements',[20] cúl and cúil (meaning recess). Toner goes on to say 'it is now believed that *cúil* is the more common of the two elements in townland-names.'[21]

Cathair Céirín (stone fort of the plaster/poultice), Caherkereen: local tradition has an ancient hospital located here. Also in this townland is a large stone chimney (known as the Simné) which is visible for miles around. This is a remnant of an Elizabethan fortified mansion; such houses 'were erected ...mainly during the late 16th and early 17th centuries ...'[22] O'Donoghue links this mansion with the Baldwins. However, no knowledge of it survives in local folklore but it has become mixed up with the original placename so that a vague tradition of it having been a hospital has arisen. Cathair Céirín may suggest the ancient residence of a *Leagha* or physician.

Príomh-Thus (first settlement), Prohus: the name suggests the first settlers in what would have been heavily wooded countryside located here. Appropriately, the last remaining aboriginal woodland in the parish is Prohus Wood. Murphy mentions that the older generation of 19th century native Irish speakers pronounced it 'Prío-thus'. O'Donoghue derives the name from 'Pruches' meaning a cave or vault. Presumably he gets his derivation from a mixing of 'pruch' and 'puatais', each meaning a hole in the ground. T.S. Ó Máille also takes 'Prohus' (for the three instances of the name in Co. Cork) to come from 'pruch'.[23] In his 1837 account of Co. Cork, Samuel Lewis noted an extensive slate quarry in Prohus, along with veins of copper ore.[24] As Murphy was familiar with the original local pronunciation his derivation is the more authoritative.

Cathair Deaghaidh (stone fort of [clan] Deaghaidh), Caherdaha: there are three ringforts in this townland. The name derives from the Clann Deaghaidh, as we have noted. Following their expulsion from Ulster, they were supposedly based around the district where Castleisland, Co. Kerry, is now. They are also associated with Gleann Deaghaidh, south of Dunmanway and Caherconree, seat of Cúroí Mac Dáire, one of their most famous leaders, on the Dingle peninsula. It is also, as we have seen, referenced on Corrin Hill near Fermoy. A cave in Caherdaha is known as 'Leaba Dumha Dara' and was reputedly used by this mythical hero when out hunting. Dumha Dara was presumably of the Clann Deaghaidh. His name is still recalled in the neighbouring Glenflesk area in Co. Kerry where the phrase 'adharca Dumha Dara' survives to denote a discomfort or irritation. A poem composed by a Cill na Martra poet of the 20th century as part of a local 'contention of the bards' speaks of going
        'Ó Leaba Dumha Dara
        Go Carraig a' Bhainbh.'

Caol Fuinseann (narrow strip of the ash trees), Kylefinchin: 'Caol' usually refers to a fertile strip of land beside a stream or river. As the topography here doesn't lend itself to this meaning, the term must refer to a narrow band of ash trees originally to be found there.

Sean Bhaile Sheáin (Seán's old habitation place), Shanballyshane: OS gives Shanvallyshane.

Drom Réidh (smooth or level ridge), Dromreague: at a bend in the road here is Lúibín na gCorp. The derivation of this name in reference to an ancient battle has already been given. In more recent times, that is from the Penal era to the advent of motor transport, funeral processions from the church at Cill na Martra to the graveyard at Dundareirke were on foot. There were two large stones by the roadside here until very recent years. During Penal times the coffin would be placed on these for the priest to read the last rites as he could not do so at the grave-side because the cemetery was next to the Glebe-house of the Established Church. The tradition of laying the coffin on the stones continued in post-Penal times, to allow a change of pall-bearers for the remaining journey.

Páirc an Oileáin (field of the island), Parkanillane: perhaps named for the occasional flooding of the Toon River which causes 'islands' to appear. Another possibility comes from the practice of the Normans during their conquest of new lands of establishing moated sites for defensive purposes until they had time to build a castle or more permanent stronghold. This may be how Oileán Chiarraí became Castleisland. In Co. Cork one of these sites has been identified and excavated at Ballyheeda. When the Normans were expanding from their settlements in the good land of the Lee valley, the de Cogans extended their sway to include Macroom and the lands along the tributaries of the Lee. The Toon valley would have been a likely route of ingress for them.

Seantoir (Glebe lands), The Glebe: here was situated the Established Church and Rectory, next to the ancient cemetery of Dundareirke. This townland dates from 1591 when 40 acres were given to the first Protestant Rector appointed to the parish.

Bruachán (little brink or edge), Brehaun: O'Donoghue derives from 'Brachán', a place of soft ground.

Drom Óinigh (bountiful ridge), Dromonig: probably so called from the produce grown in kitchen gardens for the nearby castle of Dundareirke; the legendary hospitality found there had the poets name the area Fearann Dhruim na Féile, the lands of the ridge of hospitality. O'Donoghue derives from 'Drom Uaithne', meaning green ridge; but local pronunciation of the name shows this cannot be right.

Drom a' Gharraí (garden ridge), Dromagarry: again, probably named for being a kitchen garden for the nearby castle.

Inse an Bhreacháin (river inch of the trout), Inchibrackane.

Curraichín (little marsh), Curraheen.

Ráth Laoich (ringfort of the hero or champion), Raleigh: the noted scholar John O'Donovan gave the derivation from Ráth Liath, the grey fort, when he worked on the ordnance survey of the parish in 1842. He was in error here as local pronunciation does not support this.

Inse na hAmhraí (river inch of the elegy), Inchinahoury: this is Murphy's derivation and he points out that 'amhra' was always a poetic elegy. As this is a masculine noun the derivation appears to be incorrect. O'Donoghue gives it as '…of the hill brows', but the plural cannot be grammatically correct. However, 'abhra', feminine genitive singular 'na h-abhraí', means a poem[25] – so perhaps Murphy's derivation is not so wrong.

An Ceann Droma (the head or beginning of the ridge), Candroma.

Garraí an tSasanaigh (Englishman's garden), English Garden:

probably refers to a garden plot laid out in English style by the local landlord, Baldwin. Here also is located Poll na gCnámh, hole of the bones, so named during famine times when cattle belonging to the landlord were killed and eaten by the starving people. The bones were buried to remove evidence of the 'crime' and so avoid legal retribution.

Ráth Una (Una's ringfort), Rahoonagh: O'Donoghue gives Ráth Thamhnaigh, ráth of the clearance or green spot in waste ground.

Cúil a' Bhuacaigh (recess or sheltered place of the bleacher), Coolavokig: there is a tradition of some type of woollen mill being located here at one time.

Conor Murphy's point about local names being indicative of the continuity of native culture is well taken. Diarmuid Ó Murchadha has pointed out (in the case of the neighbouring parish of Uíbh Laoghaire), 'the very place names …reflect its imperviousness to outside influences. In the Normanised or semi-Normanised parts of Ireland the use of *baile* (or *–ton*) to denote a farmstead/ holding spread like wildfire across the landscape … [here] the most frequent initial place-name elements are *Daire* or *Doire/Doirín*, an 'oakwood' or 'grove', and *Gort/Goirtín*, a 'plot of land'. Other natural features such as *Inse*, 'river meadow', *Carraig*, 'rock', …*Drom*, 'ridge', are also in evidence.'[26]

These placenames give an insight into the history and culture of Cill na Martra. As Prof. Dáibhí Ó Cróinín has written: 'of all our historical evidence, place names are often the most valuable …'[27]

Notes and references

[1] P., 'Extracts from an Antiquary's Note Book', 1910, p.17

[2] Philomena Connolly, *Medieval Record Sources*, 2002, pp.38-39

[3] Seán Ua Súilleabháin, *op. cit.*, p.653

[4] P. Connolly, *op. cit.*, p.38

[5] *Diocese of Cloyne AD 2002*, p.29

[6] Paul MacCotter and Kenneth Nicholls (eds.), *The Pipe Roll of Cloyne (Rotulus Pipae Clonensis)*, 1996, p.60

[7] *ibid.*, p.61

[8] In this section the work of Conor Murphy, 'Parish of Cill-na-Martra: Its Ancient Topography and Traditions', Part I, 1897 and (to a lesser extent) Bruno O'Donoghue, *Parish Histories and Place Names of West Cork*, 1983, were useful.

[9] Murphy, *op. cit.*, Pt. I, 1897, p.275

[10] *ibid.*

[11] Paul Walsh, *Irish Leaders and Learning through the Ages*, ed. Nollaig Ó Muraíle, 2003, p.404

[12] Eugene O'Curry, *Lectures on Manuscript Materials of Ancient Irish History*, 1861, p.590

[13] Art Ó Maolfabhail, 'Baill Choirp mar Logainmneacha', 1987, pp.76-82

[14] John Canon O'Hanlon, *Lives of the Irish Saints*, 1875-1903, Vol. 5, pp.114-17

[15] Power *et al.*, *op. cit.*, p.314

[16] Colmán Etchingham, 'Pastoral provision in the first millennium: a two-tier service?', 2006,p.86

[17] Michael Slavin, *The Ancient Books of Ireland*, 2005, p.2

[18] RIA 23. P 1, f 948

[19] John Lyons, 'Local Names. Topographical and Personal', 1894, p.133

[20] Gregory Toner, 'The Backward Nook: *Cúil* and *Cúl* in Irish Place-Names', 1996-7, p.113

[21] *ibid.*

[22] Mulligan, *op. cit.*, p.28

[23] T.S. Ó Máille, 'Irish Place-Names ending in *–AS, -ES, -IS, -OS, -US* ', 1989-90, p.138

[24] Samuel Lewis, *Lewis' Cork*, 1998, (first published 1837), p.113

[25] See Alexander McBain, *An Etymological Dictionary of the Gaelic Language*, 1911, reprinted 1982

[26] Diarmuid Ó Murchadha, 'Uíbh Laoghaire In The Seventeenth Century', 1993, p.218

[27] D. Ó Cróinín, *op. cit.*, p.22

CHAPTER 3: ST. LACHTAIN

The original Fire Kindling Stone, an Old Red Sandstone rock from which Cloch Adhnadh or Clohina takes its name, still remains. The Editors' Notes to Conor Murphy's article in 1897 relate that it was still known then as the Fire Altar[1] and posit a druidical origin for the site. It can be argued that this is the most significant historical site in the parish as the parish owes its very existence to this site; for it was here that St. Lachtain, patron saint of Cill na Martra, had his ecclesiastical site.

According to Murphy, St. Lachtain 'erected this church about the middle of the sixth century …it stood within a few yards underneath the Bealach Feabhradh, the ancient highway of Cill-na- Martra.'[2] The Gobán Saor is, almost inevitably, reputed in folklore to have been the builder. No trace, apart from a mound of stones, now remains of Cill Lachtain as the site was cleared in the early years of the 19th century on the instructions of the clergy.

Murphy, on whose family farm it stood, claimed to have been able to trace its outline in the latter part of the 19th century, especially when the site was being tilled, (a technique which modern archaeology also attests to). He gives its dimensions as 60 ft. by 18 ft., built on an east-west orientation with an entrance in the west. Modern scholarship shows this to have been the traditional form of early churches, which was abandoned only in post-Penal times.

It was reputedly plundered by the Vikings but restored and

continued to flourish as an ecclesiastical centre up to the 16th century. In John O'Donovan's edition of the *Annála Ríoghachta Éireann* or Annals of the Four Masters we find recorded for the year 836 AD: ' Cealla laichtíne Inis Cealtra, i Cill Finic do losccad le Gallaibh'.[3] In Hogan's *Onamasticon Goedelicum*, St. Lachtain's churches – Cealla Laichtene – are enumerated as follows: 'c. laichtene; i. Laichtin's churches; cella Laichtene; St. Lachtine's churches were Achad-úr (Freshford, c. Kilk.), Bealach-abhra in Muscraidhe, c. Cork, Lis-Lachtin at Ballylongford , c. Kerry, Fm. i. 456'[4] [Fm = Annals of the Four masters].

O'Donovan's edition of the Annals gives the same listing for the churches of St. Lachtain in a footnote to the text: '*The Churches of Laichtene* – the Churches of St. Lachtin were Achadh-Ur, now Freshford, in the county of Kilkenny; Bealach-abhra in Muscraidhe, in the county of Cork; and Lis-Lachtin at Ballylongford in the north of the county of Kerry.'[5]

We know from the *Cogadh Gaedheal re Gallaibh* that in 812 a fleet of 120 Viking ships raided as far as Valentia before being defeated by the Eoghanacht Locha Léin. In 845 and 857 the monastery of Inisfallen and the surrounding district were raided. So we know the Vikings were raiding throughout the south in the first half of the 9th century.

Tradition in Freshford holds that St. Lachtain founded a church there in 622 AD. In 1100 this was replaced by a larger stone structure with a Romanesque doorway which has an inscription in the 'Ór do .../ Pray for ...' format seeking prayers for Niamh, daughter of Corc, and for Mathgaman O Chearmaic and Gille Mocholmoc O Chearmaic for whom the church was built. A prayer is also sought for Gille Mocholmoc O Ceannucain who made the church. In the 1730s the church was completely rebuilt and now stands as the Church of Ireland by the village green. The Romanesque doorway remains, one of only two such extant (the other being in Clonfert). A Conservation Plan for this important structure has been drawn up by the Heritage Council. According to one tradition it was St. Comgall of Bangor who directed Lachtain to Achadh-Úr. There is also a well dedicated to Lachtain adjacent to the village. His name lives on in St. Lachtain's GAA club which figures prominently in Kilkenny hurling.

Lislaughtin of Ballylongford is primarily noted now for the Franciscan Friary founded by John O'Connor Kerry (usually dated to 1478), probably on the site of an ancient foundation of which Lachtain was patron. Fr. Paul Walsh noted that on the flyleaf of a manuscript in the Royal Irish Academy (MS 23 D 17), known as O'Clery's Book of Irish Pedigrees after Friar Micheál Ó Cléirigh, there is a list of Franciscan foundations in Ireland:

'An bliadhain d'aois ar ttigearna i ndernad na máinéstracha so síos í n-onoir do Dhia agus do Naom Fran ...1470 m.[ainistir] Lesa Laichtnin ...'[6]

The *Leabhar Meic Cárthaigh* (Book of the MacCarthys) notes the death in 1192 of Fingin Lici Lachtain mac Mec Carthaigh. It also notes for the year 1209 that Fingin Mac Diarmada Mic Cormaic (Mac Cárthaigh) 'do marbadh la hIbh Suillibháin ag Lic Lachtain.' In 1588 an Elizabethan Fiant (5177 [6609]) leased to Sir Edward Denny 'the church of Lislaughty ...and the circuits of the house of Franciscan friars of Lislaughtie' along with the land belonging to it.

The saint is also closely connected with other foundations in what are now counties Cork, Clare and Limerick.

In Co. Clare[7], Kilfarboy (now Miltown Malbay) has a well dedicated to him, as does Kilnamona (modern parish of Inagh-Kilnamona), along with Kilmurry parish. T.J. Westropp records (following Bruodin) that the shrine of St. Lachtain's arm was 'preserved at Kilnamona before it was removed to Lislachtin in County Kerry.' The Ordnance Survey Letters for Co. Clare (1839) state that 'St. Lachtainn the only saint remembered' in the parish of Kilfarboy. It also notes that his well in the churchyard was still 'much frequented' and that his feast day was the same as Achad-Úr, 19 March.

Westropp also notes a well dedicated to him at Stacpoole's Bridge, which was renamed St. Joseph's Well in 1839. It is reputed that a number of such changes were made in west Clare in the 19th century where Joseph was substituted for the traditional Lachtain.

Kilfarboy derives from Cill Feabhradh. Perhaps the name originated with Lachtain being known as the saint from Bealach Feabhradh or maybe the highway ran through north Cork and touched on south Limerick before going on to Clare, linking some of the sites associated with Lachtain.

There is also a St. Lachtain's Well, sometimes also called Tobar na nAingeal, north-east of Lisdoonvarna at Kilcorney. It was reputed to have a cure for eye ailments.

In Clare local history the Cineál Baoith, associated especially with Kilnamona, were reputed to have had a special veneration for the saint. Giollachtain or Giolla Lachtgi, meaning servant or follower of Lachtain, were traditional names among them and in west Clare in general.

The saint is also associated with Killougheen near modern Newcastlewest in Co. Limerick. The townland of Killougheen was originally not part of the parish of Newcastle but part of Ardagh parish; being annexed to Newcastle in 1841 by the then bishop of Limerick, Dr. Ryan. Ardagh, where the Ardagh chalice was discovered in 1868, had been an important centre from medieval times until the Norman foundation of Newcastlewest. One of the largest hillforts in Ireland, covering 52 acres, is located in the nearby townland of Ballylin.

In neighbouring Manister parish is found a well also dedicated to Lachtain. Toberlaghteen is located in the townland of Knocknagranshee. Up to modern times devotions were held on

19 March and the well was particularly associated with eye ailments; a motif linking wells dedicated to this saint. There is also a local tradition that the well moved to its present location from another site after being profaned. This well, dry since 1955, is enclosed by a beehive type construction. Noted Limerick folklorist Kevin Danaher recorded in 1955 that he found an inscription on the wall of the construction dating it to 1791. The parish name suggests an ancient monastic foundation.

Lachtain's name is also connected with Ballyhea in north Cork. In 1440 Pope Eugenius IV confirmed a grant by the Lord of Fermoy, Maurice de Rupe (Lord Roche), to the Abbey and Rectory of St. Lachtain's Parish Church in Ballyhea, vacant by the resignation of John Walshe.

In modern times his fame has spread further. The Irish summer college in Inis Oirr is named Coláiste Laichtín Naofa. However, the saint had no connection with the Aran Islands, the name being given to the summer college by an enthusiastic Clareman.[8]

Francis J. Byrne noted that an 'interesting feature of the ecclesiastical scene is the number of houses founded by saints of west Munster origin in the sixth and seventh centuries across the centre of Ireland …'[9] Byrne also refers to what he terms a 'curious document' preserved in the Laud genealogies[10] which purports to be an account of a west Munster synod held in the 6th century. Various saints, including Lachtain, Ciaran and the two Brendans (Kerry and Birr) are present. The cause appears to be the transfer of allegiance by various tribal groupings from the Eoghanacht Locha Léin to Cashel, no doubt reflecting a geopolitical shift at that time. The various saints mentioned have the role of taking the oath on behalf of their own people. Thus Mo-Lachtóc (the hypocoristic form of Lachtain's name) swears on behalf of the Múscraighe. Byrne notes that the saints mentioned are the representatives of the west Munster foundations across the middle of the country. The precise significance of this is now lost to us. What is clear is the political and social importance of Lachtain as a representative of the Múscraighe in the geopolitics of ancient times.

It is interesting that the diocese of Killaloe which takes in most of Co. Clare also extends to Birr in Co. Offaly, taking in parts of Limerick, Tipperary and Laois as well. As 'Birr lay on the very boundary between Munster and the Southern Uí Néill'[11] we can look at the Laud MS., also known as the West Munster Synod, as a type of peace treaty guaranteeing boundaries against incursions; not unlike what the UN seeks to effect in trouble spots today. Prof. T.M. Charles-Edwards has shown[12] that in the 9th and 10th centuries the provincial and dynastic boundaries were relatively stable and peaceful, showing that a peace treaty or *cairde* must have been in force for a long period of time. The church would have been important in overseeing this – the UN of that time – with the major monasteries of Clonmacnoise, Durrow, Clonfertmulloe and Birr etc., along with their lesser and dependant houses making a type of early medieval 'green line'. In fact these monasteries may have been peace enforcers as much as passive ceasefire observers. The Annals of Ulster, for instance, record the battle of Móin Choisse Bláe in 760 AD between the communities of Clonmacnoise and Birr.

Osraige, where modern Co. Kilkenny now lies, was at this period part of Munster, (something that would lead to many battles over the following centuries as kings of both Munster and Leinster sought to establish their authority there). Indeed, the various Annals show that in the late 700s the most active military leader in Munster was the king of Osraige, Anmchad mac Con Cercae, who engaged in a series of wars with Leinster.

It might be proposed, therefore, that Lachtain's association with foundations from Clare to Kilkenny forms part of the political guarantee of boundaries at the time. Just as a UN peace keeping force is composed of troops from outside the warring nations, a saint from outside the contending neighbouring tribes was needed. As a peace keeping force has to be credible in terms of armaments etc., so also the saint had to be credible in terms of his standing in the popular mind. Lachtain of the Múscraighe obviously had that status; he is mentioned in an ancient poetic text *The Miracles of Senan* (St. Senan) along with Mac Léinín (St. Colman of Cloyne), Molaga, Finnchu of Brigown, Cainneach, Comgall, Mochua, Cuimin, Ailbhe and Ruadhan of Lorrha, a veritable who's who of saints of the south of Ireland, showing he was recognised as being a high status saint. His status as a Munsterman was not in doubt, however, as we shall see later.

Lachtain is also associated with the parish of Donoughmore in Co. Cork and the neighbouring parish of Grenagh, where the parish church is dedicated to him. Tobar Lachtain is located in Grenagh parish, in the townland of Garryadeen. The antiquarian Richard Caulfield visited this well in 1864. He noted that, despite its Irish name, the local people 'call it St. Joseph's Well.' The similarity with what happened in Clare at around that time suggests an abandoning of traditional saints' names, starting before the Famine but probably accelerated by the trauma of that event, to be replaced by biblical ones. It is noteworthy that the chapels of ease in Donoughmore (at Fornaught, built 1840) and Grenagh (at Courtbrack, dedicated in 1871) are both named for St. Joseph while the main parish churches are dedicated to St. Lachtain. It is also noteworthy that Grenagh and Donoughmore were united as a single parish up to 1790.[13] The reason why Joseph was chosen as the biblical personality to supplant Lachtain can be explained by their sharing a feast day. The feast of St. Joseph the Worker was created in the 20th century as part of the Left versus Right conflict in European politics. From the early Church the feast of St. Joseph was celebrated on 19 March, which is also St. Lachtain's Day.

Lachtain is reputed to have founded a monastery at Donoughmore, which in ancient times had its own high cross. A ruined former Church of Ireland church in the old cemetery at Donoughmore Cross marks the site.

The well at Garryadeen is enclosed on three sides and covered by a corbelled roof. Local historian Brian Gabriel gives its dimensions as, 'about 1.75 metres high with a 1metre high opening giving access to the water within. An ancient hawthorn bush overhangs it and on it are many votive offerings'.[14] When the Cork Archaeological Survey visited the site in 1983, a wooden cross was noted and photographed on the corbelled roof.[15] When Caulfield visited in 1864, he noted that 'about seven years ago', a wooden crucifix was set up at the well. He also noted that on St. Lachtain's day, an old woman attended at the well to place white stones in the water, 'as forfeits for those who come for cures in this place.' The modern archaeological survey found quartzite pebbles, along with coins and broken delph, at the bottom of the well.

Local legend has it that the well was originally at Knockyrourke in Donoughmore parish but removed itself to Garryadeen following an 'unclean act' offensive to the saint — a young woman washing either her feet or her clothing in the water of the well. This reflects an identical motif to that of Toberlaghteen in Manister parish.

St. Lachtain's site in Clohina was probably already sacred before the coming of Christianity, the name Cloch Adhnadh or Fire Stone suggesting druidic associations. Conor Murphy describes six fonts from the site.[16] He also describes a remarkable incident when two others were found. In 1851, a woman visiting from Kerry had a series of visions, he relates, about two wells. She described their location so accurately that Murphy's father, John Murphy, who was we are told 'of an antiquarian turn of mind', was able to identify the exact spot. Having cleared away several inches of sod, he discovered two hollows in the rock-lodge, round in shape and being roughly two feet or so across and three feet deep. They are best described as being like two halves of an egg. Muintir na Tíre erected a cross to mark the spot in 1950.

Murphy tells that while the exact location was up to then unknown, local tradition told of their existence in the general area as Lachtain was reputed to use it as a retreat from the bustle of his monastic foundation. The tradition of the founder having a nearby retreat to which he would repair for meditation from time to time is well attested for early Irish saints. Thus Jonas in his account of Columbanus tells us that the saint found a hollow in a rock some miles from the foundation at Annegray, from which he drove a bear, and made it 'a resort...to which he might repair for meditation.'[17]

St. Lachtain's Well

Tobar Lachtain is in the townland of Ballyvoige. Now overgrown, it was a place of pilgrimage within living memory, and was covered and roofed like the well in Grenagh. A short distance from it is another well, Tobar na bPian, which -as the name suggests -was reputed to give relief from pain, especially bone pain but also eye ailments (to continue the motif associated with wells dedicated to Lachtain).

In 1938, as part of the Schools Folklore Project, Neans Ní Shúilleabháin collected from Conchubar Ó Éaluighthe of Ballyvoige, who was then over 70 years of age, the tradition that Tobar na bPian had moved to its present position from another spot.

Associated with the site of Tobar na bPian is a cillín. According to Conchubar Ó Éaluighthe, the well was also known as Tobar Cillín, and was named after a Naomh Cillín, a first cousin of Lachtain. Devotions were held at Tobar na bPian or Tobar a' Chillín as it was also called, up until the 1950s. The 'rounds' were performed for two Sundays and one Friday, or two Fridays and one Sunday. It was recorded from Conchubar Ó Éaluighthe that, 'le h-ais an tobair tá cathair agus tá sé ráidhte gur roilig a bhí ann fadó.'

Before Tobar Lachtain came to its present condition the entrance to the well is reported to have been spacious and capable of accommodating four people in a beehive type construct. There were three rough openings or windows to admit light to the well. There was a flagstone or *leac* about 16 yards west of the well. This construction seems to match that at Grenagh exactly.

The pattern here was held in June. Large crowds attended and races were held from Ballyvoige to Dromreague. However, in the 19th century faction fighting caused the clergy to suppress the tradition. Fr. Lee of Macroom came to reside on this farm and he denied access to the site. As Conchubar Ó Éaluighthe put it: 'tá sé ráidhte gur Meitheamh an tSamhraidh a bhí an patrún ann. Do thosnuigh na daoine ar bruighean le céile…'

There is also a Tobar Lachtain at the Clohina site. Conor Murphy tells us the site at Clohina was cleared by order of the clergy about the year 1835. 'The ancient cemetery of Clohina, near which St Lachtain's church stood, was a very large one…

there were three principal tombs, one of which was open, and contained four underground vaults or dumai with a passage in the centre dividing them.'[18] The main entrance from Bealach Feabhradh was at the north-west corner, with another entrance at the west leading to the well and church: 'At this back entrance stood two pillar stones, placed about five feet apart and nine feet high. One of these pillar stones is said to have had an Ogham inscription on it, which, at the time they were removed, the Rev. Michael Lane, who was then curate at Ballyvourney... tried to decipher.'[19]

Murphy mentions six 'fonts', or bullaun stones, which were on the site, one of which remains with two others being preserved locally at Renaniree church. He had in his possession in San Francisco a 'small round stone' from the site inscribed with a bent-arm cross or swastika. This ancient sun symbol could well have been from a pre-Christian usage of the site.

That St. Lachtain was an important Irish saint is shown by the reference to him in the literature. The *Feilire hUi Gormain* mentions 19 March as his feast day, as does *O'Clery's Calendar*: 'Lachtain, mac Toirbéin, abb Achaidh uir i n-Osraighibh, ugus ó Bhealach Feabhrath Anno Domini 622.'

The *Annals of the Four Masters* note: 'Aois Chríost, sé chéad fiche a dó ...S. Lachtnain mac Torbén, abb Achaidh uir, décc 10 do Marta'.

The noted Gaelic scholar John O'Donovan corrects this in his edition:
'The age of Christ, 622...St Lachtnain, son of Torben, Abbott of Achadh-Ur, died on the 10th [recte 19th] of March'. [20]

O'Hanlon in his *Lives of the Irish Saints*, says that Colgan's MS of the Annals had the correct date, 19 March .[21] He is also noted in the *Martyrology of Tallaght*, *The Book of Leinster*, and the

Corpus Genealogiarum Sanctorum Hiberniae. The famous hagiographer, Jean Bolland, SJ, noted Lachtain in his massive work in the 1600s. For 19 March, he writes: 'In Hibernia S. Lactini Episcopi & Confessoris'. He continues: 'Sanctus autem Lactinus ex parentum generositate nobilitatus de regione Munsteria a fuit ortus: haec autem regio Corcagiae civitate est vicina. Pater S. Lactini Torphurus appellabatur, & mater eius Senecha vocabtur.'[22]

Lachtain, then, is said by Bolland, - working from ancient manuscripts, many of which are no longer extant – to have been a Bishop and Confessor (a common formula used when describing saints) and to have been of parents from the Munster nobility, specifically from the Cork region. His father was Torphurus (Torbén) and his mother was called Senecha.

O'Hanlon, holds that Lachtain 'was a member of Corpre Musc's illustrious family, belonging to Muskerry, in the county of Cork'.[23]

Hagiography tells us that while St. Molua was at St. Comgall's monastery in Bangor, an angel appeared to him to forecast Lachtain's birth. A miracle is ascribed to him while he was still in the womb, foreshadowing his sainthood. An old, blind man named Mohemeth received a supernatural light which gave him visions of Rome and other foreign places. Mohemeth was present at St. Lachtain's birth. There was no source of water nearby so the old man took the baby's hand and traced a sign of the cross in the earth with the baby's finger. Immediately a spring burst forth. Mohemoth then baptised the child. Later Lachtain was brought to another saint for baptism but the holy man had a vision telling him the sacrament had already been received; he then went to prophesy the future sanctity of the child. Other childhood miracles such as surviving poisonous food, curing his mother of disease and banishing a plague infecting cattle are ascribed to St. Lachtain. When he reached the age of 15, his guardian angel, Uriel, supposedly directed him to St. Comgall's monastery at

Bangor; there St. Molua was his teacher. It is noteworthy that while Killoughteen may have once been in the parish of Ardagh, as we have seen, St Molua is the patron saint of the parish and he has two wells dedicated to him located there.

It is also worth noting that, again as we have already seen, Lachtain was known as Mo-Lachtóc. Both the name Lachtain and this hypocoristic, or pet-name, form of it come from the root 'Lacht' meaning milk – here meaning 'milk white'. Both the name (-ín) and the hypocoristic form (-óc) end in a diminutive which is affectionate in nature. The name means '(My) little milk-white one' and reflects both affection and sanctity; compare the many saints named Colm or Colmán (one of whom of course is the patron saint of Cloyne diocese in which Cill na Martra is located) where the white dove image is used to signify sanctity. Charles-Edwards has stated that 'Old Irish is rich in pet names. One type of pet name, such as MoLua or Do Bécóc, is apparently restricted to monks.'[24] Mo-Lachtóc falls comfortably into this category.

Colgan in his *Acta Sanctorum Hiberniae* recalls Lachtain's political role in Munster. He quotes St. Cuimin of Conor (Coindeire) telling how Lachtain stood in defence of the army of Munster. The Bollandist account quotes the same attribute: '… in vigilis stare pro Momomiorum defensione.'[25] This tradition is remembered still in the seanfhocal from Co. Clare: 'Luighim fé ghrásta Dé ach fágaim Lachtaín naofa ina dhiaidh air', uttered when faced by insuperable odds and meaning 'I bow before the grace of God but leave Lachtain to avenge me.'

O'Hanlon records that 'Not only during his life, but even after the death of St. Lachtain, miracles were wrought through his intercession.' He specifically mentions a well devoted to the saint at Liosnasciath [Lisnaskea, Co. Tipperary] which was renowned for cures. Lachtain was also associated with the parish of Donoskeigh, also in Tipperary. Given the political considerations outlined above, it is noticeable both of these are near Cashel, the ancient political capital of Munster. The memory of Lachtain in both these areas went with the suppression of patterns in the 18th century. In a pastoral letter dated 17 May 1797 the then archbishop of Cashel Thomas Bray excommunicated not only those who would attend the pattern of the well in Donoskeigh but also any who provided food or drink for them. So concerned was he to root out the pattern that the pastoral specifically condemns not only those who would misbehave but also any who would 'perform any work of penance, any pious act, or any sort of religions duty', at or near the well.

This now almost forgotten Tipperary association was also politically important as it gives a connection between Lachtain's cult and the area where the historically important monastery of Tír Dá Ghlas (Terryglass) was located. In a footnote to his work,[26] O'Hanlon recounts an incident recorded in a manuscript in the Royal Irish Academy where a priest of Tír Dá Ghlas was struck by a man named Dermod in Carlow. A sacred relic was broken in the attack. For this sacrilege a fine was levied, payable to the monastery and to Lachtain.

Lachtain's fame for miracles after his death is recognisable in the name of the parish, Cill na Martra. 'The Church of the Relics' must have become a place of pilgrimage for the pious and especially those seeking relief from various afflictions. Tobar Lachtain and Tobar na bPian must also have been such centres.

The main relic was without doubt St Lachtain's arm. We know this because the shrine for housing the relic – known as Lámh Lachtaín – is still extant and now in the Treasury Room of the National Museum. Raghnall Ó Floinn notes that 'the shrine of St. Lachtain's Arm ... can be dated to between the years 1118 and 1121 through the names of Munster kings recorded on its inscription.'[27] He also states that it is no coincidence that many of the surviving shrines and reliquaries can be dated to this period. It was a time of upheaval and change in both religious and secular structures. Political dynasties and ecclesiastical patronages were being formed. Thus, 'during the eleventh and twelfth centuries a number of Irish saints' remains were exhumed and placed in ornamental shrines or reliquaries.'[28] In this context, the name Cill na Martra suggests that this was the location of the saint's grave.

Lámh Lachtaín

This image is reproduced with the kind permission of the National Museum of Ireland

At some later time the shrine was in the care of the O'Healy family, erenaghs of Donoughmore, a foundation also associated with Lachtain. Smith's *History of Cork* records regarding Donoughmore that 'The patron saint was named St. Lachteen, and some years ago the parish priest kept here a brazen hand, as a holy relic, by which the people swore upon all solemn occasions, but this hand was removed by one of the titular bishops of Cloyne.'[29] This was the Protestant Bishop Synge.

We know from an account by Bishop Bennet of Cloyne (1794-1820) that this happened in 1639. Synge fled during the 1641 uprising and the shrine came into the possession of Edmund Fitzgerald. It appears to have been returned to Donoughmore but about 1750 passed into the hands of the Fountain or Fontaine family, who relocated it to the family seat at Norfolk, England. Andrew Fontaine exhibited it at the Society of Antiquaries in 1829. In 1884 it was sold at Christie's for 410 guineas and repatriated to the Royal Irish Academy from where it passed on to the National Museum in 1890.

The reliquary itself takes the form of a 15 inch long wooden case made of yew, in the form of a hand and forearm. It was made to contain the actual relic of the saint's arm, now sadly no longer extant. The reliquary is covered by bronze gilt, inlaid with silver. It may be that the yew-wood casing predates the bronze reliquary encasing it. It is certain that the relics of St. Lachtain were being venerated centuries before the making of Lámh Lachtaín as the very name Cill na Martra attests to this. It may be that the relic was removed by the MacCarthys, overlords of the district at that time, for the express purpose of encasing it in the shrine.

The reliquary has four inscriptions on it, in the standard 'Ór do...' (a prayer for...) format.

1. (d)o chormac mc meic carthaighi do rigdanu mumand
2. or do tadc mc meic c(a)rthaigi do rig
3. (o)r do diarmait mc meic denisc do comarba
4. (o)r do maelsechnaill u cellachai do ardrig.

The first calls for a prayer for Cormac mac meic Cárthaigh, rígh damha or heir to the throne of Munster. The second calls for a prayer for Tadhg mac meic Cárthaigh, the king. A prayer is also sought for Diarmait mac meic Denisc, comharba or successor of Lachtain. The final prayer is for Maelsechnaill Ó Ceallacháin, Árd Rí of Ua Eachach Mumhan, who had the shrine made. We know from the Annals that this Maelsechnaill died in 1121, while Tadhg became king in 1118 so we can date the shrine to the early part of the twelfth century, between 1118-1121. This same Maelsechnaill is associated by Michelli with Petrie's crozier of St. Mura, also housed in the National Museum.[30]

Frank Mitchell describes Lámh Lachtaín as 'a metal fore-arm with bent fingers, decorated in the Hiberno-Viking style; the upper end of the arm is closed by a circular cap.'[31] Ó Floinn sees the influence of the Crusades in the development of arm reliquaries in Europe, one of the earliest of which was Lámh Lachtaín. Ó Floinn thinks it 'closer to contemporary Byzantine than to western European examples.'[32] However, Griffin Murray sees German influence in the style of the arm. He states that 'the earliest extant arm-shaped reliquaries came from Germany and it is highly likely that the concept of arm-shaped reliquaries was directly imported from there to Ireland.'[33] He mentions the 11th century Irish monasteries in Germany -the Schottenkloster – in this regard, and also notes that 'the early date of the reliquary suggests that it was one of the first, if not *the* first, to be produced outside of Central Europe.'[34] Wallace and Ó Floinn state that Lámh Lachtaín is among the shrines that 'best preserve the stylistic details and overall integrity of the eleventh and twelfth centuries.'[35]

Lámh Lachtaín is unique among European arm reliquaries in that it depicts a closed fist. The top of the fist is considerably worn in comparison with the rest of the arm, probably indicating it was the custom to hold the top of the shrine while taking an oath on it.

The circular cap at the base of the arm has a decorated flat rim, at the centre of which is a round aperture. This is not visible in the Museum, as the arm is standing upright on its base. A thin silver plate was at some later time, fixed inside this aperture, itself having a smaller aperture at its centre. A bronze strap, part of which remains, was rivetted inside this. 'The strip was obviously intended to hold some object which filled the circular aperture; a lens of rock crystal is an obvious suggestion.'[36] This would have allowed the devout to view that actual relic encased in the reliquary. Mitchell tells us there is an engraving of a watercolour of the complete reliquary in a volume entitled *Instrumenta Ecclesiastica*, held in the library of the Society of Antiquaries in London. The engraving dates from 1839, so the shrine was complete at least up until that late date.

Prof. Pádraig Ó Riain, one of the foremost scholars of Irish hagiography, holds that St. Lachtain is a purely mythical figure (as is, he also holds, St. Finbarr). In a 1978 paper he takes as his starting point that ' the more one studies the record of the Irish saints…the more apparent it becomes that many must have been formerly the subject of local, pagan cults.'[37]

Given that Lugh was probably the most important pre-Christian deity, Ó Riain concludes that the 'god survived under the modified, but none the less homonymous, forms of his name.'[38] As the north Munster area from the Ballyhoura hills up to the Slieve Blooms has connections with St. Molagga (of Templemolagga), Molua (of Clonfertmulloe) and Lachtain (of Freshford, etc), who was also *comharba* of Molua by some traditions, Ó Riain conflates these three into one, and collapses that one into the pagan Lugh. He takes the existence of Lámh Lachtaín as confirmation of this, it being a continuation of the motif of Lugh Lámhfhada for Ó Riain. He does concede at the end of the paper that 'the case will never be fully proven.'[39]

Ó Riain's arguments here are less than convincing. As we

have seen, the arm-shaped reliquary has its origins in medieval Europe, not pre- or early- Christian Ireland. Ó Riain himself allows that 'coincidences of festival must seem a more valuable proof of identity...the feast of the deity fell... on *Lugnasad*, August 1st, which, according to the principal Irish calendars of saints, was the later the feast of Lachténe.'[40]

However, this is untrue. March 19 is, as we have seen, St Lachtain's feast; with 26 June also connected with him. His principal feast of 19 March was held in the widely scattered areas throughout Munster and Ossory associated with him. Lachtain's feast is given at 19 March in the *Féilire hUi Gormain* and also in *O'Clery's Calendar*.

St. Molua is the main patron of the parish of Ardagh and has two wells dedicated to him there. In contradiction of Ó Riain's thesis he is not conflated with Lachtain, who also has connections with the area as we have seen, in local tradition. Crucially, vis-à-vis Ó Riain, Molua's feast is celebrated here on 4 August while Lachtain's is not.

While Ó Riain might have been trying to apply the medieval philosophical proposition of William of Occam (known as Occam's razor) which says the entities should not needlessly be multiplied (entia non sunt multiplicanda praetor necessitatem) he falls to what we may call the historical corollary of Occam's Razor – entities should not unnecessarily be conflated.

A better historical understanding might be gleaned from the notion of *paruchia* in the early Irish church. Following J.F. Kenney, Prof. Dáibhí Ó Cróinín proposes that 'the Irish churches appear to have been transformed into a quite different but distinctive organization... the *paruchia* was not a traditional unity with fixed boundaries, for the monastic churches comprising it might be widely scattered.' [41]

While this view might be challenged by other scholars such as Colmán Etchingham,[42] Ó Cróinín's view of *paruchia* along with the West Munster Synod, already alluded to, explains both the dispersal of sites dedicated to St. Lachtain within Muskerry and the modern diocese of Cloyne, and also those sites along the border of ancient Munster, from the Shannon to the Slieve Blooms. That the notion of extended *paruchia* is tenable is shown by, for instance, looking at later Gaelic Galloway in Scotland where the Premonstratensian monastery of the aptly named Soulseat Abbey (founded c.1148) was directly subject to Prémontré Abbey in Picardy and politically and financially supported by Fergus, Lord of Galloway, and his lineage. [43]

Notes and references

[1] Murphy, *op. cit.*, Pt. I, 1897, p.289

[2] *ibid.*, p.277

[3] John O'Donovan, (ed.), *Annála Ríoghachta Éireann: Annals of the Kingdom of Ireland*, 1856 (2nd edition)

[4] Edmund Hogan, *Onamasticon Goedelicum: Locorum et Tribuum Hiberniae et Scotiae*, 1910, p.196

[5] J. O'Donovan (ed.), *op. cit.*, p.456, footnote 'e'

[6] Paul Walsh, *op. cit.*, pp.567-68

[7] Information from standard works on Clare history by James Frost, *The History and Topography of Co. Clare* and T.J. Westropp, *Antiquities of Co. Clare*. Both texts are reproduced on Clare Co. Library website www.clarelibrary.ie

[8] I am grateful to An tUas. Caomhán Ó Conghaile of Ennis for this information

[9] F.J. Byrne, *op. cit.*, p.170

[10] *ibid.*, pp.216-17

[11] T.M. Charles-Edwards, *Early Christian Ireland*, 2000, p.594

[12] *ibid.*, pp.593-96

[13] *Diocese of Cloyne AD 2002*, pp.50-1; 56-7

[14] Brian Gabriel, *Muskerry News*, March 2006, p.8

[15] Power *et al.*, *op. cit.*, p.324

[16] Murphy, *op. cit.*, Pt. I, 1897, p. 278-79

[17] Benedict Fitzpatrick, *Ireland and the Foundations of Europe*, 1927, pp.52-3

[18] Murphy, *op. cit.*, Pt. II, 1898, p.17

[19] *ibid.*

[20] J. O'Donovan, *op. cit.*, pp.244-45

[21] O'Hanlon, *op. cit.*, Vol. 3, p.850

[22] Ioanne Bollando S.I., *Acta Sanctorum Martii*, reprinted 1968, pp.31-2

[23] O'Hanlon, *op. cit.*, p.845

[24] Charles-Edwards, *op. cit.*, p.5

[25] Bollando, *op. cit.*, p.33

[26] O'Hanlon, *op. cit.*, Vol. 6, p.805, footnote 26

[27] Raghnall Ó Floinn, *Irish Shrines and Reliquaries of the Middle Ages*, 1994, p.41

[28] *ibid.*, p.7

[29] Charles Smith, *The Ancient and Present State of the County and City of Cork*, 1815, p.176

[30] Perette E. Michelli, 'Fragments of a fifth crosier from Scotland', 1988

[31] G.F. Mitchell, 'The Cap of St. Lachtin's Arm', 1984, p.139

[32] Ó Floinn, *op.cit.*, p.16

[33] Griffin Murray, 'The Arm-Shaped Reliquary of St. Lachtin: Technique, Style and Significance', 2004, p.158

[34] *ibid.*, p.142

[35] Patrick F. Wallace and Raghnall Ó Floinn (eds.), *Treasures of the National Museum of Ireland: Irish Antiquities*, 2002, p.218

[36] Mitchell, *op. cit.*, p.139

[37] Pádraig Ó Riain, 'Traces of Lug in early Irish hagiographical tradition', 1978, p.139

[38] *ibid.*, p.142

[39] *ibid.*, p.154

[40] *ibid.*

[41] D. Ó Cróinín, *op. cit.*, p.147

[42] See for example Etchingham, *Church Organisation in Ireland AD 650 to 1000*, 1999, pp.107 and 168 ; and 'Pastoral provision in the first millennium: a two tier service?', 2006, *passim*.

[43]. Keith J. Stringer, 'Reform Monasticism and Celtic Scotland: Galloway, c.1140-1240', 2005, p.129

CHAPTER 4: MEDIEVAL: THE Uí FHLOINN AND THE MIC CÁRTHAIGH

'Múscraí Uí Fhloinn a tugtar ar an dtalamh ó abhainn na Druipsí siar go hIarthar Bhaile Bhúirne; *Muscraighe Mitine (Mittine, Mittaine)* a bhí air roimis seo',[1] says Seán Ua Súilleabháin, following the accepted tradition. Cill na Martra was originally known as Tuath na Dromann, arising – as we have seen- from its topography. 'After the twelfth century it was known as Tuath na n-Dromann Uí Fhloinn'.[2] Murphy goes on to bring our attention to a land-grant made by Queen Elizabeth I to Cormac Mac Tadhg mac Carthy in 1578 where the name is recorded as 'Tounedromyn Iflanlo'. The same document also lists 'Kilnamartrie' and 'Downedearegrek' [Dún Dá Radharc].

Barry O'Brien disagrees with the accepted view and claims the 'ancient district of Muskerry which was ruled by Flann, was called Muscraidhe Mitine and after the establishment or surnames it was incorrectly referred to as Muscraidhe Uí Fhloinn, implying that the clan of O'Flynn were the tribe in the district.'[3] He states this Flann to have been of the Cineál Laoghaire and quotes claims by earlier writers that the district of Tuath na Dromann originally encompassed the parishes of Kilmurry, Canovee, Moviddy and Aglish, along with Cill na Martra, Ballyvourney and Clondrohid.

O'Brien here seems to be following Jeremiah O'Mahony's history of West Cork which held that 'Muscraidhe Uí Fhloinn ... is an incorrect rendering of the Irish form of the modern name of Muskerry. Since this territory was conquered by Flann nearly four centuries before surnames were introduced, it is obviously improper to introduce the Ui or O, symbol of surnames.[4]

If we look back to the ancient genealogies (which Ireland is almost unique in having such a richness of - from 'genealogies alone we can recite the names of more the 12,000 persons living in Ireland from before AD 1100'[5]), we may find a resolution to this contradiction.

The *Leabhar Muimhneach* [Book of Munster] contains a genealogical poem of 126 stanzas written by Cathán Ó Duinnín in 1320 which traces the Cineál Laoghaire. The eponymous Laoghaire was son of Criomthann of the Uí Eachach Mumhan. Laoghaire had three sons, one of whom was Flann Lua, named after the River Lee, from whom descends the Uí Fhlainn Lua. This Flann Lua had four sons, among them Donnghal and Tuathal. Each of these is recorded as having five sons. Among Donnghal's sons was another Laoghaire, from whom descend the Uíbh Laoghaire. Among Tuathal's sons was Maothagán, from whom descend the Uí Mhaothagáin. Both the O'Learys and Mehigans are still closely associated with the neighbouring parish of Uíbh Laoghaire; here also is found Oileán Uí Mhaothagáin, the only crannóg in Co. Cork

A brother of the original Laoghaire, son of Criomthann, was Aodh Osraigheach. He had two sons, among whom was Cairbre. He had a son Clairneach ar Clairíneach [the Crippled]. This Clairneach had three sons, among whom we have Dunlang. He had a son Elathach, who had a son another Dunlang (or Dunland). He in turn had a son called Ainbhleithe, who had a son named Flaithnia. This Flaithnia had five sons, among whom was Flann from whom descend the Uí Fhloinn.

It is interesting to note that another son of Clairíneach was called Sealbhach. Among his four sons was Maolodhar, who himself had five sons, one of whom was named Buadhach [the victorious]. From this man descend the Uí Buadaigh. Baile Uí Bhuaigh is a townland in the parish of Cill na Martra.

We can see that the genealogies, which though partly myth also contain history, hint at a connection between the parish and surrounding area with the descendants of Criomthann for over a millennium. Even if we can never resolve the issue of which Flann (a name which means 'blood red') the name Uí Fhloinn comes from, we can see they both derive ultimately from the same blood-line.

John O'Brien, later Bishop of Cloyne, published an Irish dictionary in Paris in 1768. In the entry for the word 'Flann', he tells that it was the Uí Fhloinn who built Macroom castle in 1199.[6] Perhaps more tellingly, the *Annals of Inisfallen* record that in the year 1212, 'Mac na Sethar Ua Flainn do marbad do Chormac Líathánac'[7] [Cormac Liathanach (MacCarthy) killed Mac na Sethar O'Flynn] showing that the O'Flynns and the MacCarthys were even then in contention in the politics of west Munster. That the Ó Floinn were associated with Muskerry is shown by the earlier entry for 1115 which refers to the death of 'Mc hu Fhlaind', whom we know from the Annals of the Four Masters to have been Murchad, Lord of Múscraighe ('Murchadh Ua Flainn, the son of Flannchadha, Lord of Muscraighe, were slain').

The balance of the historical evidence, therefore, is that the term Múscraí Uí Fhloinn, and hence Tuath na Dromann Uí Fhloinn, does reflect historical reality and we can agree with Conor Murphy that: 'The O'Flynns were the ancient rulers over Múscraidhe Mitine, i.e., both baronies of Muskerry in the county Cork'.[8] These O'Flynns he goes on to say, were a branch of the O'Flynns of Arda whose main seat was Ardagh or Ardea castle and lands in west Cork. That the O'Flynns of Arda were a leading dynasty in the politics of the day, is shown by an entry in the Annals of Inisfallen for 1057, that 'Hú Fhlaind Ardda killed

Ua Mútáin, erenagh of Cork'. It is not surprising, therefore if a branch of the dynasty held lands in (or even all of) Muskerry.

The fact that Múscraí Uí Fhloinn refers to the Uí Fhloinn and not O'Mahony's Flann Lua can be shown by the fact that Muskerry did not in the early days of Múscraí Mitine extended south of the River Lee where Uí Fhlann Lua was situated (as shown on the Carew map in *Pacata Hibernia*[9]). This area was added to Muskerry as late as the Norman era when the resurgent MacCarthys, following the battle of Callan Glen, disposessed the de Cogans who had been granted the cantred of Musgraidhe Mittaine by King John in 1207. As the de Cogans had extended their holdings south of the river, the MacCarthys annexed those to Muskerry also. That the Lee was an ancient line of division is shown by the fact that Cill na Martra and the district north of the river are in the diocese of Cloyne, while Uíbh Laoghaire and the district south of the Lee are in the diocese of Cork – the diocesan boundaries being more reflective of ancient political divisions than the modern counties.

The tradition that has the Uí Fhloinn building Macroom castle also has them building Dundareirke castle. This castle, or more correctly tower-house, was built on the main Drom or Ridge running through the parish, contiguous to the ancient highway, Bealach Feabhradh, hence the name 'Fort of the Two Views'. In the tradition of Gaelic hospitality of the time, this obviously stood out as the area around it became known as Fearann Dhruim na Féile [The Land of the Ridge of Hospitality].

O'Brien held 'it appears as though the castle were erected on the site of an ancient fort or Lios'.[10] It is likely that the Uí Fhloinn had their stronghold at this lios – hence the reference to Dún rather than Caisleán or Cloch in the name – with the tower-house being built at a later time by the MacCarthys. Tower-houses would apppear to be too late an addition to the landscape for the O'Flynn era. Current scholarship holds that tower-houses in Co. Cork can be divided into two chronological groups, those built in the 15th century and those built in the 16th century or later.[11] It is notable that the nearby castle at Carrigaphooka is attributed solely to the MacCarthys.

Smith, in his *History of Cork*, credits the MacCarthys with the building of the castle. When he visited it in c. 1748, he described it as 'an high square building, having 70 stone steps to the battlements; adjoining to it, stood some modern buildings, now in ruin; here were large gardens and orchards also destroyed.'[12] This last remark recalls the nearby townland names Drom a'Gharraí [Garden Ridge] and Drom Oinigh [Bountiful Ridge] . Smith tells us Dermot Mac Carthy forfeited the castle in the 1641 Rebellion.

The account of the buildings around the castle is in accord with contemporary evidence about tower-houses. In 1591 a German traveller in Ireland, Ludolf van Munchclausen, recorded that Irish nobles built residences in the 'form of a tower surrounded by a wall. Yet they do not live in those but keep them as fortresses. Nearby they keep a house, badly built unlike our farmhouses, where they light a fire in the middle.'[13]

Intriguingly, Smith also adds to his account: 'a little to the north is the ruined church of Kilnamartery'.[14] This suggests that there was a Catholic church dating from early and certainly pre-Penal times near the castle and almost certainly associated with it. Smith's reference cannot be to the Church of Ireland building as this was south of the castle and was itself reputedly built with stone from the castle.

We saw when treating of St Lachtain that the religious axis of the district swung from the west (at Clohina) to the east (Dundareirke) in early medieval times with the falling into disuse of Cill Lachtain and its burial ground and the opening of a graveyard at Dundareirke (which is still in use today). This change was probably connected to political changes; probably the establishment of a political/military stronghold at Dún Dá Radharc by the O'Flynns.

Conor Murphy tells us that a large portion of the castle collapsed during the night sometime about the year 1820, making a tremendous noise that was heard over a wide area. James N. Healy gives 1833 as the year of the collapse but elsewhere follows Murphy closely. He also infers from the name that it stood on the site of a former 'dun or earthen ring fortress, which may have been the O'Flynn site...'[15] Healy also gives the name as Kilredagh castle 'from the name of the district'. Healy is here following Lewis who in 1837 wrote: 'the Castle of Kilredagh stands on a lofty hill and commands the passes of both the rivers which bound this parish. It was very strongly built, and remained totally entire till 1833, when a considerable part fell.'[16] Lewis also gives 'Kilnamartin' as an alternative name for 'Kilnamartry'. Neither Kilredagh or Kilnamartin are names now known in the district. In the prospectus that Lewis issued to raise subscriptions to fund his book he promised that 'several persons of competent talents' were employed in collecting from the most authentic historical works 'materials relative to each place'.[17] It would appear that Lewis was misled by an Elizabethian scribal error in Fiant 5333(4302) of 1589 which outlines the granting to Cormac McDermod (McCarthy) of Blarney of various lands including 'Twhonedromen ... Kilnemartine, Downedericke'.[18]

THE MicCÁRTHAIGH

According to the Annals, Cárthach – from whom sprang the MacCarthys – was burned to death in 1045. He was king of the Eoghanacht of Cashel. Following the death of Brian Ború in 1014 the political scene in Ireland reverted to turmoil, with a handful of powerful families tussling for the High Kingship. The main protagonists were the O'Briens of Thomond and the Uí Néill. Turlough Mór O'Connor, King of Connacht, took advantage of the strife to stake his own claim. In a cynical political move, which shows that 'divide and conquer' was known long before the Tudors, he supported Tadhg MacCarthy as a rival of the O'Briens in Munster. In 1118 he helped Tadhg become king of Deas Mumhan, thereby putting an enemy to the rear of his opponents the O'Briens of Tuadh Mumhan. As William F.T. Butler, who made a detailed study of the MacCarthys which included access to documents destroyed in 1922, says: 'This is the true beginning of the kingdom of south Munster and of the power of the MacCarthy family.'[19]

There is an indirect association between this Tadhg and Cill na Martra; he is the Tadhg mentioned in the inscription on Lámh Lachtaín, which (as we have seen) allows us to date it.

At the coming of the Normans, Dermod son of Cormac was king of Desmond. In 1171 he submitted to Henry II in Waterford. He probably saw this as an astute political act which would give protection both from the invaders and from traditional Gaelic rivals. However, six years later Henry granted the Kingdom of Cork to Fitzstephen and Milo de Cogan.

In 1185 Dermod was killed by Theobald Walter (ancestor of the house of Ormond which would feature for centuries as a rival of Desmond). Dermod's son, Dómhnall Mór na Cuirre (as the Keating *Genealogies* refer to him), reigned until his death in 1206. His brother Finghín came next; the Annals tell us he was killed by the O'Sullivans in Uíbh Ráthach in 1209.

Following Dermod's death in 1185, Prince John gave the territory now called North Tipperary to his killer Theobald Walter; South Tipperary was given to Philip of Worcester. The Eoghanacht Caisil, that is the MacCarthys, the O'Sullivans, the O'Mahonys and their followers were displaced and migrated to the south-west where they carved out new territory for themselves by force of arms and subjugating or expelling the incumbents there.

The Normans also expanded along the river valleys and fertile lands, expelling the natives. It is likely that it was around this time the O'Flynn's lost Tuath na Dromann, most probably being expelled by the de Cogans who came along the Lee valley and then along the fertile banks of the Sullane into Macroom and adjoining regions. We know for instance that the O'Herlihys of Ballyvourney, erenaghs of the church lands of St Gobnait's, came to an agreement with the de Cogans when they introduced the Norman system of church governance. This allowed the O'Herlihys to maintain their connection with St Gobnait's for many centuries even though the de Cogans granted the church and tithes of Ballyvourney to the Norman foundation of the Preceptory of St John of Jerusalem at Mourne Abbey.[20]

Whether expelled by Norman or Gael, the result was the same for the aboriginals:

> 'in some cases, such as the O'Sheas in Iveragh, and the O'Floinns in Muskerry, the former owners disappear from the rank of land owners.'[21]

The MacCarthys consolidated their new position and set up the lordship of MacCarthy Mór, which became very powerful – not just among the Gael but among the Normans as well. This was shown in 1261 when Finghín MacCarthy defeated the Normans at Callan Glen near Kilgarvan with great slaughter and ended their attempts to conquer the MacCarthy lordship.

Finghín's cousin Dómhnall Rua had fought alongside the Norman Geraldines at Callan. He not only survived the defeat but went on to become king of Desmond (as his father Cormac Fionn, who died in Mashanglass Castle, had been) when Finghín was killed by de Courcey while attacking Ringrone castle and Finghín's brother Cormac, who was his immediate successor, was killed in another major defeat of the Normans at Mangerton the following year. In fact he had benefitted hugely from the defeat at Callan, as the military tide was now seen to turn against the Normans. As Hanmer put it is his *Chronicle:* after Callan, 'the Carties plaied the Divells in Desmond' for 12 years. The MacCarthys under Dómhnall Rua now began to conquer territory from the Normans.

It is most likely that it was at this time that the MacCarthys came into possession of the territory of Muskerry, including Tuath na Dromann. The *Annals of Inisfallen* tell us that in 1261 they burned Macroom Castle – 'Caslean Mugi Cromtha ... do loscudh do Dessumin.' In 1352 Cormac, then head of the MacCarthys, took the government side against his kinsman Dermot Mac Dermot MacCarthy, who was an ally of the Earl of Desmond. In return Cormac received a grant from the crown of extensive lands 'which were to become the foundations of the lordships of Muskerry and Coshmang.'[22] As late as 1439, the last of the de Cogans, Robert son of Geoffrey, granted to James, Earl of Desmond, all his possessions, including 'Flanluo' and 'Mustrylyn' [Múscraí Uí Fhloinn] but these were 'almost certainly no longer in possession of the Cogans at the date of the grant.' It would appear that the de Cogans felt the lands were still theirs but the MacCarthys were actually *in situ*.

The system of land tenure practiced by the MacCarthys in Muskerry helps to confirm this. As a writer in *An Músgraigheach* noted:
> 'An socrú do dhein na Carrthaigh i Músgraighe b'é an t-aon tsocrú amháin i measc Gaedheal é go raibh cosmhalacht aige leis an nós feódach do thug na Normannaigh leo anall ó Shasana.' [23]

Butler concurs: 'Muskerry has this peculiarity that it represents the nearest example to anything like a feudal lordship which we find among the native Irish. The cause of this seems to be that the lords continually increased their territories at the expense of their English neighbours, the lands thus won they kept mainly in their own hands.'[24]

It wasn't only at the expense of the English that the MacCarthys expanded. Their Gaelic neighbours also suffered. They crossed the Lee to annex territories from the O'Mahony's of Ifflanloe [Uí Flannlua]. Butler tells us that in 1600 there was still a distinction between 'old Muscrie' north of the river and the annexed territories south of the Lee.[25]

Butler notes that 'Either through deliberate policy, or by a series of lucky accidents, rule passed for over two centuries directly from father to son.'[26] This uninterrupted sucession can be seen from Dómhnall Rua who died in 1302 to the Dómhnall who died in 1508. The MacCarthys therefore avoided at least some of the internecine strife which brought down so many other powerful Gaelic clans. However, as part of this system of succession, perhaps as a safety valve to avoid internal strife, 'the younger sons of the head of the house obtained for themselves in each generation extensive districts as subordinate lordships, and transmitted them to their descendants, who in some cases broke away from subjection to the senior line.'[27]

There were two aspects to the MacCarthy polity:
1. Defined territories transmissable to the descendants of the holder
2. A large degree of independence from the senior line of MacCarthy Mór; not full independence but perhaps analogous to a federal rather than a unitary state (the Lord of Muskerry could and did become MacCarthy Mór).

Dermod, son of Cormac Mór (who died in 1359 according to the *Annals Of Loch Cé*), was the first Lord of Muskerry so recognised. By the 16th century at least six sub-septs had developed, including Sliocht Thuath na Dromann

The genealogy of the Sliocht is given in *An Leabhar Muimhneach*:

> 'Geinealach Cloinne Cárthaigh Tuaithe na Dromann annso: Domhnall, mac Diarmada, mic Domhnaill, mic Fínghin, mic Domhnaill Óig, mic Domhnaill, mic Diarmada, mic Domhnaill mic Feidhlime, mic Diarmada Móir Mhusgraighe, *ut supra*.'[28]

In the *Carew MS* [29] it is recorded that 'Phelim, taniste to his brother Cormocke L. [Lord] of Muscrye 3 years he caused his nephew Dermod McTeg to be murthered for which fact he and his posteritie were disenabled to be the Lds. [Lords] of the countrye, but had the lands of Twonedromon given unto them'. As we have seen, this Phelim was Feidhlimid, son of Diarmuid Mór of Múscraighe. Feidhlimid became Lord of Muskerry on killing his nephew. However, the *Leabhar Muimhneach* relates that in 1382 vengeance caught up with him: 'Feidhlime ... do marbhadh a Musgcroidhe le Muinntir Mhurchadha'. The Uí Mhurchú were retainers of the MacCarthys and were presumably acting on behalf of the rest of the MacCarthys.

Dundareirke castle was the seat of Sliocht Thuath na Dromann and the tower-house was probably built by them on the site of an earlier Dún of the O'Flynns, which may also have been fortified by the de Cogans. This latter is unlikely as the de Cogans probably confined themselves to Macroom castle. The Tuath na Dromann sept were subject to their kinsman the

Lord of Muskerry. There is no surviving documentation giving the political structures of the Lordship but we can learn from details supplied by government papers. Thus an Inquisition (17th of James I) tells us that Charles (Cormac) MacCarthy, son of Sir Cormac MacDermod, had, *inter alia,* when he became heir to his father as Lord of Muskerry:

> 'and out of the rest of the lands of Towneydromane, containing in all 19 ½ ploughlands,[30] the yearly rents as by way of rent charge of forty-two in-calfed cows, and two- third partes of a cow, ten muttons and vid. Sterling.'[31]

He also held a number of 'marriage cows', payable out of Tuath na Dromann:

> 'And so often of the said Charles or his heirs shall prefer annie his daughters or his sisters in marriage there is issuinge out of the said nynteen ploughlands the number of sixteene cowes with a proportionable number of labourers, garrans, worke and wages as hath antiently bin allotted and divided upon the territories of ould Muskrie, and also to pay to the rising out, and general hosting proportionably for his Majesty's service.'[32]

Another inquisition (12th of James I) tells us that two ploughlands owned by Dermitius MacDowell Oge Carty (Dowell here is probably an error for Dómhnall; giving the name as Diarmuid MacDómhnaill Óig Mac Cárthaigh), who died as a rebel in 1601, were in the townlands of 'Coolekeadigan, Inshinegaple, Gortnimeale, Inshindowrigg.' Gortanimill is instantly recognisable and Inshindowrigg is probably Insenahoury; however

Coolekeadigan [Cúil Céadagáin] and Inshinegaple [Inse na gCapall] are names no longer extant. It is noticeable that the two recognisable townlands here are not contiguous. These two ploughlands paid to the Lord of Muskerry as follows: 15 cows and two sheep for annual rent; two cows to help to marry the Lord's daughter; the labour of four oxen and four horses on everyday from 1 May to the last day of July; and when the Lord built a castle or stone structure the payment of three parts of a 'faber lignarior' and three parts of a 'faber lapidarior' for the same period. These latter terms can be interpreted as a carpenter and stone-mason from the Latin for wood and stone respectively.

The Lords of Muskerry progressively moved closer to the crown administation. This was a political move to maintain their lands while outflanking not only their enemies but also their nominal overlord and kinsman, the MacCarthy Mór. This was a traditional tactic of all branches of the MacCarthys going back, as we have seen to the time of Henry II. This jockeying for position both within the MacCarthys and between them and their neighbours and rivals is very like the dynamic within and between mafia families in modern times, with bosses of 'families' jockeying for position with each having an eye to becoming the 'capo di tutti capi.'

In 1565 Domhnall MacCarthy Mór – described by one writer as being neither a sturdy rebel nor a loyal subject – made a surrender of his title and lands to the crown, in order to consolidate his own position. These clan lands were then re-granted to him personally along with an English title, Earl of Clancar. The account of this investiture is described in a 'thick and appparently contemporary MS. volume in the British Museum'[33] entitled *'The Booke of Heraldrye and other thinges togither withe the Order Coronacons of Emperours, Kinges, Princes, Dukes, Byshoppes, Earles, and other Estates: with the Maner of their Buryalls and Enterrmente'*.[34] As this account had been given in print only once before, and that almost exactly a century ago, it is meet to reproduce it here:

> 'The Manner of Creating of Mac Artye more of Ireland from a Lorde Barron of Valencia to a Earle.
>
> The xxiii Daye of June Anno dni 1565 et de regni regine Elizabeth VII Syr Donnell Macke Carte more knight of Palles Baron of Valencia & Earle of Clyncarre in Ireland was first created Baron of Valencia and then Earle of Clyncarre by the Q[ueen's] Matie in the chamber of presence in Westmynster palace and the said Baron was invested in a kyrtell of scarlett and a barons hoode of scarlet and his ow[n] e girdell aboute hym and was led by the Lord Wyndsoure and the L. Mountioye in their robes of Scarlet and hoodes of Barons. The L. Wentwoorthe carrieng the mantell of the said Sir Donnell betwixte his Armes before the said newe Baron invested in his Robes of pliament. Garter principall King at Armes in England in his Coate of Armes, going right before they said Lorde Wentwoorth, holding and showing vpright in the L[ette]res patente roled vpp with the Queenes Ma^{ts} greate seale in greene waxxe & all the hyeraulds and pursewants of Armes in theire Coats af Armes before the said garter p[re]ceeding through the great chamber with the sounde of the Trompette, And So to the chamber of presence where the Queenes most excalent Matie accompaned wth all hir Nobles and L. of hir privie counsell & ladyes, and Thembassadoure of Spayne & his nobles and gentleme[n] were: Hir Matie sytting vnder the clothe of Estate. And after the first Entrance into the chamber of P[res]ence place being made & the Queenes Matie once p[er]ceaved Three Reverances humblie made by tharforenamed Baron & the other Lords app[roa]ching nigh to the Queenes hignes Garter vpon his knee kyssed the said L[ett]res patente & del[iv]yued the same vnto the Q. Matie who receaving the same delyued it vunto Sir william Cicell principall Secretary to bee red aloude, the said Baron during

the tyme of the reading of those Lres patente kneeling apon his knees before hir Matie. And when it came to the Investing of his Mantell hir Matie tooke the saint from thafforesaid L.Wentwarth and therew^th Invested the said new Baron of Valencia and aftrewards delyeud vnto hym his Lres patente who receaving the same with all reue[r]nce at hir gracs hands aftre humble thancks given to hir ma^tie arose vpp and all humble made to hir highness retourned in deue forme of his Entrance as afforesaid being led by thafforenamed Barons vnto the place afforesaid and wer hooded and the said Barons Invested them selves also. Then the said Baron of Valencia did also invest hym self in the Kyrtell of an Earle as the maner ys.

> M^d that the Robes of Baronye wherewith the said Sir Donnell m' Cartye more was that daye Invested did apptaigne and belonge vnto the Lorde Northe'.

The Muskerry MacCarthys were particularly adept at courting English support. As Ring points out, an 'example highlighting their close association with the Government was the manner in which they tended to Anglicise their names. They began changing Donal to Daniel, Cormac to Charles...'[35]

Sir Cormac Mac Teige was Lord of Muskerry during the Desmond Rebellion. He gave such service to the government at that time that the Lord Deputy, Sydney, called him 'the rarest man that ever was born of the Irishry'. In 1578 he had been re-granted by Fiant almost all of Muskerry, including Tuath na Dromann.

'Grant (under queen's letter, 22 May, xix) to Cormock mc Teige Mc Cartie, of the Blarnye, co. Cork, knt.; of the whole country of Muskrie, and the territories of Iveleary,Twonedromyn,Iflanlwo,... Mocrompe...Kielnemartrie, Downedeareyrck... Ballywornie ...'[36] Allowing for Elizabethan scribes being unfamiliar with

Irish, the list of names is almost instantly recognisable, with (for our purposes) Tuath na Dromann, Macroom, Kilnamartyra, Dundareirke and Ballyvourney standing out.

He had surrendered these lands the previous September. Under English law the Lordship should have gone to Cormac Mc Dermod, eldest son of Sir Dermod Mc Teige McCarthy, the previous lord. Sir Cormac used the Gaelic Tánaiste system to get the title himself. As soon as he was recognised by his own people as Lord he then 'adopted the "surrender and regrant" policy so as to retain the Lordship and lands in his own family.'[37] The English administration took a price; not all of the lands in the surrender were given back in the regrant. Some were given to, among others, Sir Lucas Dillon. Dillon amassed a large amount of land throughout the country by featuring in Fiants. He was made Chief Justice for Common Pleas in 1559, and was an ancestor, on the female line, of Oliver Plunkett.

Cormac Mc Teige died in 1583. In his will, which he says he made 'for conscience sake'[38] he reverted to Gaelic tradition and left the lordship and lands firstly to his Tánaiste (and brother) Callaghan; on Callaghan's death they were to go to Cormac, son of his eldest brother who had been Lord of Muskerry before Cormac Mc Teige; after this Cormac's death the lands and title were to pass to Cormac's brother Teige; finally and only on the death of Teige were the lands and title to go to Sir Cormac Mc Teige's own son, also Cormac.

However, his nephew Cormac persuaded Callaghan to stand aside (while retaining Castlemore and Carraignamuck castle, along with the land he held as Tánaiste) and claimed the title for himself under English law. To preserve his tenure of the title and lands this Cormac McDermod then did a 'Surrender and Regrant', in Fiants dated 1589:

'Surrender by Cormac Carty fitz Derby alias Cormac mc

Diermod mc Teig McCarty of the Blarny...Twonedromen ... and the lands of Blarny...Kilnemarterie, Downdearyke ... Ballivourny... Clonedrohid ... with the intentions of their being regranted.
Signed Cor Carty. Dated 2 May xxxi'.

On 9 May he was regranted 'the whole country of Muskerry and the territories of: ... Twohenedromen ... and all the lands rents and services in Blarny ... Kilnemartirie, Downedericke ... all of which the grantee had surrendered by his deed; also half of the goods of felons and outlaws, of all fines ... To hold forever by the twentieth part of a knight's fee. Rent £5 13s. 4d.'[39]

This taking of the government side left the MacCarthys in control of Muskerry while other great Gaelic and Norman landowners such as the Earls of Desmond were reduced and their lands expropriated.

Followers and Pardons
One curious sidelight thrown up by the will of Sir Cormac Mac Teige, and the usurping of it by Cormac Mac Dermod by his 'Surrender and Regrant' of 1589 is the documentation drawn up by English government sources when Cormac Óg, son of Sir Cormac and putative ultimate heir, fought to vindicate his own rights under his late father's will. This documentation was preserved in the *Carew MS*.

In describing 'The Septs of the Carties' it lists:
'Clan Cormocke Oge   15 ploughlands
Slught Decane   17 do.
Slught Tuonedromin   18 do.
Slught Cloghroe   10 do.

> Sept of Clonfaddagh   1 do.
> Sept of Shanekillie   5 do.'

Shortly after this it lists:

> 'Riordans   9 ploughlands
> McSwynes   5 do.
> Morohoes   - do.
> Callaghans   3 do.
>
> These be followers in Muscreye'[40]

The number of ploughlands for Morohoes [Murchús] is not decipherable but, as Diarmuid Ó Murchadha points out,[41] the list is in descending order of the number of ploughlands so four is probably the correct number here.

The O'Riordans, McSweeneys, and Murphys were hereditary followers of the Mac Carthys and were probably introduced into the area when the MacCarthys expelled the de Cogans. Indeed these family names are still strongly associated with Cill na Martra, showing a settlement pattern with roots in medieval times.

The MacSweeneys were originally 'Gallóglaigh', that is professional soldiers (of Norse rather than Gaelic extraction) introduced into Donegal from Scotland in the 13th century. They later came to Munster in the employment of the MacCarthys. Their epiphet 'Mac Suibhne na dTua' [of the battle-axes] comes from their military avocation and not from 'na dTuagh' as Conor Murphy mistakenly concludes.[42] 'The other 'followers', the O'Riordans, O'Murphys, etc, either performed certain duties, military and domestic, in the household of the lord, or tilled his lands. It was from dependants of this class, not belonging to the body of the clan, that the great chiefs drew much of their strength.'[43]

These 'followers' were probably pushed to the south and west at the same time as the MacCarthys were dispossessed of their tenure of Eoghanacht Caisil by Norman encroachment. Thus

Diarmuid Ó Murchada writes: 'Migrating as they did, to southwest Munster over which, from 1261 onwards, the MacCarthys became undisputed lords, it is no surprise to find that from the 14th century onwards almost all references to the Uí Mhurchadha are in connection with the MacCarthys, whose loyal followers they became.'[44]

Ó Murchadha goes on to state that: 'One stronghold from which they are conspicuously absent is the castle of Dundareirke (par. Kilnamartery) in the territory called Tuath na Dromann.'[45] He bases his conclusion on a modern audit of gravestone inscriptions where Dundareirke graveyard is deemed to have conspicuously few Murphy headstones in comparison with other MacCarthy stronghold locations. He goes on to recount the killing of Feidhlimid of Sliocht Thuath na Dromann by the Uí Mhurchada in revenge for the murder of his nephew, hinting perhaps that the Uí Mhurchadha were not followers of the MacCarthys of Tuath na Dromann thereafter.

However, his evidence here is less than convincing. Inscribed headstones for the common people did not come into being until the 19th century and even into the 20th century in some cases. Up until that, most graves were marked by a simple, uninscribed stone at the head of the newly turned grave. There may well be many such Murphy graves in Dundareirke cemetery. Indeed the land adjoining the cemetery was owned by a family of that name at the end of the 19th and beginning of the 20th centuries. The ancient burial ground of St Gobnait's in Ballyvourney has numerous Murphys, many from Cill na Martra, buried by the south-east corner of the ruined church. Many others are buried in the graveyard in Kilnamartyra village. We do know from the 1766 census, the earliest census for the parish, that the number of Murphys then recorded was actually greater that the number of MacCarthys.

It might also be mentioned that Dundareirke (like St

Gobnait's), being an ancient graveyard preceding the Reformation, was used for both Catholic and Protestant burials. The prescence or absence of older headstones in both cases is more an index of the material wealth of individuals and families in the 18th or 19th century rather than an indicator of population in earlier eras.

Ó Murchadha does point out that the 'Fiants of Queen Elizabeth...are a mine of information for family and placenames in Elizabethan times.'[46] The word 'Fiant' comes from the Latin *Fiant Litterae patentes...*'; they were warrants from the crown directing the issue of letters patent under the great seal. Many of these are lists of names of people granted pardons and they list a number of people in Cill na Martra.

Fiant 6467 (5327) lists pardons to 'Cormock m'Dermod M'Carthy of the Blarnin, co. Cork, esq' and to his followers, *inter alia:*
'Finine m'Donell oge M'Cartie, of Dundirick ... Dermod m'Donell oge, of Dundirig, gent, Dermot m'Donogh M'Donell, of dromonie, gent.,... Teige O Connell, of Dundirig, yeoman, Donell O Connell and Morrice O Connill, of same, yeomen, Donogh and Teige O Monighan; Awliffe O Shighan, Shane O Connill, Teige M'Shiarhie, Donogh O Connill, Donell M'Dermod, Brien and William O Connill, Teige M'Shiarhie, Donogh O Connill, Donell M'Dermod ...Shane O Clerie, Dermod M'Shane, Dermod O Lwensie, Dermod M'Donell, Tirlagh M'Cunnigan, John M'Dermod, Owen M'Morrogh, Cnogher M'Teige, Teige O Lenhsie, Donell O Gallvaine, of same...'[47]

This shows that names like Murphy (Morrogh), O'Connell, Moynihan (O Monighan), Sheehan (O Shighan) and Lynch (O Lwensie / Lenshie) which are still numerous in the area have been associated with it since the 16th century at least. It is also noticeable that Christian names such as Donal, Denis (Donogh / Donnchadh), Amhlaíobh (Awliffe/Humphrey), Tadhg, Diarmuid and Conchobar (Cnogher) are as popular today as then.

Fiant 4826 (4110) grants a 'Pardon to …Finin m'Dermod M'Carty, of Twonydromyn, yeoman'. The same pardon included 'Philip O Swlivan, of Ardea, gent., in co. Cork'.[48] As we shall see later, the path of the O'Sullivan Beares and Dundarierke would cross again during the Nine Years' War.

In 1587, a pardon was granted to 'Art O Lery, alias O Lery, of Carrignigillach, co. Cork, gent,…Owni m'Donill M'Cartie, of Kilmartery, Conogher and Dermod m'Teig m' Donogho O Lerie, husbandmen, Awliffe m'Donill O Swilliuan, of same, gent.,. …'[49] This was not the first time Pardons had linked the O'Learys of Carraig na nGeimhleach to Cill na Martra. On 8 May 1573, a pardon was issued to 'Cormuck m'Teig M'Cartie, of Blarny, co. Cork, knt., sheriff of that county…Donald og M'cartie, of Kilnymartery, and Arthur O Leary, of Carignygyelagh, gentleman, … Owen m'Donill M'Cartye of Kilnymartery,…'[50]
As we shall see another Art Ó Laoghaire, outlaw, was linked with Cill na Martra in the 18th century.

This same Cormac Mac Taidhg, described as 'late sheriff of that county' also features in a pardon of 1576, along with 'Thady m'Owen M'Carthy, of Karrigfooke, same co. …Dermod m'Teige m'Dermod M'Carthy, of Kilnymartirie…'[51] As these pardons were issued off lists of names submitted to the English administration during the O'Neill wars it is not unusual to have the same individuals appearing on different pardons.

On 8 December 1586 an individual from Clohina featured in a pardon: 'Shane m'Donell O Cronyn, of Clohins …'[52]

Others appearing in pardons were:

'Teige m'Donell oge Cartie, of Toanadwin, gent.,… Dermod m'Teig O Connell, of Dundirig, Conogher m'Hurly Hierlihie, Donell m'Shane I Linshie and Teig m'Donogh

M'Donell, of same...'[53]

Following the defeat of Kinsale, various individuals from Cill na Martra who had been on the O'Neill/ O'Donnell side were given pardons in 1602-3. These included: 'Fynen m'Donell oge Cartie, Duondarreige, gent., Margaret ny Donogh, his wife, Morris O Connell, Donogh lea O Regane, Donogh oge O Miagh, Donogh O Connell, Connell m'Donnell O Connell, and Teige O Connell, of same,...'[54]

This same Fynen [Finghín] and his wife Margaret (now described as ny Donogh M'Donnell) appear in another pardon very shortly after the first was issued, along with a list of other followers including:

'Connogher m'Donogh I neale, Morris O Conill, Connell m'Donell I Connell, Dermod O Connell, Donogh m'Teige O Regane [presumably the same as the Donncha Liath mentioned above], Donogh O Connell, Donogh O Myneghane, Dermod m'Shane I Lenchie, Teige O Connell, Wm Connill, Donell O Connill, Owen m'Donogh M'Donell, Donell m'Dermody ny Donogh, and Donell m'Teige I Riourdane' all of Dundareirke along with 'Cosney M'Buelliget of Achunage [Cosnochta (Barefoot?) Mac Baothalogáin of Ahacunna], Carbery M'Buellige, John M'Gullyneane, and Dermod m'Owen M'Edmund, of same... [and] Mahowne Fitz John, of Coulvocke [Coolavokig]'.[55]

Notes and references

[1] S. Ua Súilleabháin, *op. cit.*, p.661

[2] Murphy, *op. cit.*, Pt. II, 1898, p.7

[3] B. O'Brien, *op. cit.*, p.22

[4] Jeremiah O'Mahony, *West Cork: Parish Histories and Place Names*, n.d., p.2

[5] James MacKillop, *Myths and Legends of the Celts*, 2005, p.49

[6] Ua Súilleabháin, *op. cit.*, p.662

[7] Seán MacAirt (ed.), *Annals of Inisfallen*, 1988 (first published 1944), p.340

[8] Murphy, *op. cit.*, Pt. II, 1898, p.7

[9] Reproduced in Denis Paul Ring, *Macroom Through the Mists of Time: An Historical Geography of Macroom c.500-1995*, 1995, p.63

[10] B. O'Brien, *op. cit.*, p.24

[11] Colin Breen, *The Gaelic Lordship of the O'Sullivan Beare: A Landscape Cultural History*, 2005, p.69

[12] Smith, *op. cit.*, p.182

[13] Dagmar Ó Riain-Raedel, 'A German Visitor to Monaincha in 1591', 1998, p.230

[14] Smith, *op. cit.*, p.182

[15] James N. Healy, *Castles of County Cork*, 1988, p.53

[16] Samuel Lewis, *Lewis' Cork: A Topographical Dictionary of the Parishes and Villages of Cork City and County*, 1998 (first published 1831), pp.307-08

[17] See T. Cadogan's Introduction to Lewis, *op. cit.*, p.1

[18] Kenneth Nicholls, *The Irish Fiants of the Tudor Sovereigns*, Vol. III, 1994, pp.83-4

[19] William F.T. Butler, *Gleanings from Irish History*, 1925, p.3

[20] See Pádraig Ó Maidín, 'The O'Herlihy's of Ballyvourney', *Cork Examiner*, 9 May 1972

[21] Butler, *op. cit.*, p.6

[22] K.W. Nicholls, *Gaelic and Gaelicized Ireland in the Middle Ages*, 2003, p.189

[23] 'Músgraighe Uí Fhloinn', [no author given], *An Músgraigheach*, 1943, p.4

[24] Butler, *op. cit.*, p.107

[25] *ibid.*

[26] *ibid.* p.138

[27] *ibid.*

[28] Tadhg Ó Donnchadha, *An Leabhar Muimhneach*, 1940, p.209

[29] The late Prof. Brian Ó Cuív in his catalogue of Irish MSS in Oxford refers to this MS by Carew as being completed in the late 16th or early 17th century. It is now in the Bodleian library (MS 103 5 r b). See Ó Cuív, *Catalogue of Irish Language Manuscripts in the Bodleian Library at Oxford and Oxford College Libraries*, Part I, 2001, pp.299-301

[30] A ploughland was the amount that could be tilled in a season; usually taken as 120 acres but could vary widely in different terrain. See Breen, *op. cit.*, p.221

[31] Quoted in Butler *op. cit.*, p.131

[32] *ibid.*

[33] James Buckley, 'The Investiture of Donal MacCarthy Mór with the Earldom of Clancar, A.D. 1565', 1908, p.101

[34] Egerton 2642 fol. 8

[35] Ring, *op. cit.*, p.70

[36] Nicholls, *Irish Fiants*, Vol. II, p.462, Fiant 3373 (6360)

[37] John T. Collins, 'Fiants of Queen Elizabeth relating to City and County of Cork: with notes', 1938, p.19

[38] Quoted by Butler, *op. cit.*, p.250

[39] Nicholls, *Irish Fiants*, Vol. III, pp. 83-4, Fiants 5330 (5960) and 5333 (4302)

[40] Quoted in Butler, *op. cit.*, p.117

[41] D. Ó Murchadha, 'The Uí Mhurchadha or Murphys of Muskerry, Co. Cork', 1969, p.6

[42] Murphy, *op. cit.*, Pt. II, 1898, p.7

[43] Butler, *op. cit.*, pp.121-22

[44] D. Ó Murchadha, 'The Uí Mhurchadha ...', p.4

[45] *ibid.*, p.11

[46] *ibid.*, p.7, footnote

[47] Nicholls, *Irish Fiants*, Vol. III, pp.384-88

[48] *ibid.*, Vol. II, pp.726-27

[49] *ibid.*, Vol. III, pp. 30-1, Fiant 5069 (2912)

[50] *ibid.*, Vol. II, p.294, Fiant 2264 (1837)

[51] *ibid.*, Vol. II, pp.392-93, Fiant 2941 (2348)

[52] *ibid.*, Vol. III, p.4, Fiant 4946 (4176)

[53] *ibid.*, Vol. III, p.481, Fiant 6539 (5258)

[54] *ibid.*, Vol. III, p.609, Fiant 6762 (5468)

[55] *ibid.*, Vol. III, pp.612-13, Fiant 6764 (5470)

CHAPTER 5: THE 17TH AND 18TH CENTURIES: THE NEW ORDER

The Battle of Kinsale was the turning point in Irish history; the defeat of the Irish forces there leading to the demise of Gaelic civilisation which had prevailed in Ireland for well over a millennium

The historian Don Philip O'Sullivan Beare in his *Historaie Catholicae Iberniae Compendium*, published in Lisbon in 1621, tells us that after Kinsale and the fall of Dunboy Donal Cam O'Sullivan Beare was determined to continue the fight. He sent Cornelius, the son of O'Driscoll More to Spain to seek further aid. He was also relying on Hugh O'Donnell, who went to Spain immediately after Kinsale, to raise forces there.

In August 1602 Donal Cam led 1,000 men into Muskerry to spread the rebellion and threaten Cork city. He had escaped the seizure of Dunboy as he had been at the O'Sullivan castle of Ardea on Kenmare Bay, where a ship with Spanish gold and other supplies had arrived.

O'Sullivan first took Carrignacurra castle and enrolled the O'Learys into his forces. He then crossed from Uíbh Laoghaire into Tuath na Dromann and besieged Dundareirke castle. Don Philip recounts how he set up gabions and sows – siege instruments – to force the surrender of Dundareirke. The MacCarthys of Tuath na Dromann were now enrolled into his army. He then went on the take Macroom and Carrigaphooka castles. Carrigaphooka was surrounded by a double stone wall, no trace of which now remains. Given the similarities in style and time of construction between Carrigapooka and Dundareirke it is likely that Dundareirke also had defensive walls enclosing it.

By this time Carew has arrested Cormac mac Dermod McCarthy, Lord of Muskerry, who had fought – however reluctantly, as his brother and son were held hostage by Carew – on the English side at Kinsale. Cormac's nephew Tadhg, who had been on O'Neill's side, had sought his own advantage by alleging Cormac was conspiring with the Spaniards against the English. Owen McSweeney and six other followers of Cormac's rescued him from Shandon castle in Cork and escaped into the wilds of Muskerry. There Cormac met Donal Cam and joined him in besieging Tadhg's kin in Carrigaphooka.

The Muskerry McCarthys and O'Sullivan Beare were now united, with an army of fighting men over 1,500 strong. Yet, by the beginning of October the whole effort collapsed when news arrived of O'Donnell's death in Spain. Donal Cam now realised another Spanish army would not be coming and his tactic of holding out in the fastnesses of Muskerry and Beara was doomed.

By Christmeas of 1602 Sir Charles Wilmot had brought an army of 5,000 men as far as Glengariff where O'Sullivan was camped. Leaving camp-fires burning to fool Wilmot, O'Sullivan Beare slipped away in the night for the long march to Leitrim. 'At dawn on December 1st, they moved out swiftly, lightly, and as silently as possible. Four days had passed before Wilmot advanced, not knowing the quarry had slipped through his fingers.'[1] The wounded and sick who had been left behind had bought time for for the column's escape by keeping the campfires burning. An English account of the event says of those left behind that their 'pains and lives by the soldiers were both determined', meaning no mercy was given to prisoners.

Though it was in the depths of a harsh winter and many of

those on the march were the families of the fighting men, the column of 1,000 persons covered 26 miles over rough terrain in the first day. Passing by Carriganass castle at Kealkil and through the Pass of Keimaneigh and on to Augheris on the border of Cill na Martra, where they camped the first night. Near here, probably on the following morning, 1 January 1603, Donal Cam's favourite horse, An Chearc – named for the animal's hen-like deliberate gait – was lost in a bog hole. This place is still known as Poll na Circe.

The column entered Cill na Martra at Gortnabinna, passed through Renaniree and on to the shrine of St. Gobnait in Ballyvourney. Aodh de Blácam noted that as he entered Renaniree he was close to Dundareirke and other castles 'that he had entered so few weeks before, but now they were in his enemies' hands again, and he a mountainy fugitive.'[2]

As O'Sullivan Beara made his way to the Shannon it is noticeable that the path he took went, to a great extent, from one religious site to another. It is likely that he was following an ancient pilgrim route. For a part of the march they were on the Bealach Feabhradh as they crossed the Ballyhoura Hills from which highway the hills take their name. This was a mountain section of the great ancient highway which continued to Macroom and then through Cill na Martra to link with the Bealach Mogh Ruith from Kerry, as we have seen.

1641 and its Aftermath

When the 1641 rebellion broke out, the MacCarthys at first tried to remain uninvolved. They were following their traditional policy of siding with, or at least not confronting, the government forces so as to be left in control of their lands. However, the virulent opposition of St. Leger, Lord President of Munster, to anything Gaelic or Catholic and the increasing outrages by colonists on the native population forced their hand.

Donogh MacCarthy, Lord Muskerry, initially led a delegation to St. Leger to promise to keep the peace in Munster when the rebellion had broken out in Ulster. St. Leger refused to meet them and said if he had his way he would hang the best of them.

From their initial reluctant involvement, the MacCarthys soon became centrally involved in the rebellion and the Confederation of Kilkenny which flowed from it. As a MacCarthy territory, Cill na Martra had its own part in this. In 1645 when Rinuccini, Nuncio to the Irish Confederates, landed in Kenmare he went to Ardtully castle, near to the site of Finghín MacCarthy's victory at Callan Glen in 1261. He then travelled to St. Gobnait's shrine in Ballyvourney. From there he set out for Macroom castle to join Viscount Muskerry. He went as far as Coolavokig, then following the ancient highway Bóthar na Réidh he turned north to Clondrohid where he was met by MacCarthy's son Cormac, accompanied by 500 horsemen, before proceeding on to Macroom.

With the arrival of Cromwell in Ireland in 1649 the defeat of the Irish was followed by a sustained land-grab. In the Introduction to his publication of the Civil Survey (a land survey as part of this expropriation of lands) for Muskerry (1654-56), Robert C. Simington notes that: 'By an Act passed in August 1652, it was declared that a position had been reached when a settlement of the Irish nation might be effected...'[3] It has been estimated that in 1641, about two-thirds of the land was held by native Gaelic or descendants of Anglo-Norman (i.e., Catholic) landowners. By the end of the Williamite confiscations this had fallen to one-tenth.

It may be thought that Cill na Martra remained largely unaffected by earlier appropriations as the MacCarthys almost invariably ended up on the government side. However, there were some inroads by Elizabethan settlers, as a few historicial clues attest.

We have already seen that the townland of Glebe was created in 1591 when 40 acres was given to the newly established Protestant Rector of Kilnamartyra.

The most visible clue still extant is located in the townland of Caherkereen. Known locally as the 'Simné', it is a stone chimney stack. Located on the northern slope of the main ridge which runs through the parish and is visible for miles around, not least from the main Macroom-Killarney road. It is remarkable that there is no local folklore about this structure apart from vague stories of it being some kind of hospital. These arise from the original place-name Cathair Céirín (fort of the poultice/plaster, as noted earlier) which predates this structure by many centuries. Hospitals in the modern sense did not exist in Tudor or Elizabethan times.

This chimney is the remains of an Elizabethan mansion.[4] As Prof. Toby Barnard has noted: 'Officials, anxious that Ireland should be assimilated to English ways, sought visible evidence that this was happening. Houses, in their styles and materials furnished it ... the English mission to Ireland ... insisted on such recognizable conveniences as glazed windows and fixed chimneys...'[5] The underlying logic was of extending social control by means of of a series of manorial houses, each one a nucleus of the new order which would be bounded by and give to and receive support from its neighbours. The establishment (Protestant) histories from Richard Cox in the 1680s, through Smith in the 1740s and on to Lewis in the 1830s, are really a description of country 'seats'. This can also be seen in the 1777 survey by Skinner and Taylor of the roads of Ireland; the subsequent road maps published by them in 1783 list all the gentry whose houses adjoin each stretch of road. Their map (no.176) showing the roads west from Macroom shows Ashgrove as the residence of 'Ash Esq.' Also delineated are Hutchinson of Codrum, Eyre of Mounthedges, Brown of 'Coolcour', along with Barry and Masters of Inchigeelagh and others. By the same logic, England in the early 18th century has been described as a federation of country houses.

The siting of the Elizabethan mansion at Caherkereen along the main ridge is interesting. As we have seen this had been the main artery of communication since earliest, even pre-historic times. It is reasonable to assume Macroom would have been the base from which the colonial settlers had extended, in a process similar to what we see in the West Bank and Gaza Strip today. David Dickson has noted: 'Muskerry, under the earls of Clancarthy, was slower to change, still being characterised as late as the 1680s as a 'large wooded country";[6] thus it appears the river valleys may still have been heavily forested at this late stage.

The Elizabethan settlers were probably driven out when the MacCarthys joined the 1641 Rebellion. We know from the Depositions of dispossessed settlers post-1641, that Joan Hupp, wife of John Hoop [sic] of Clogheea [Clohina] claimed there was killing 'in the highway'; and Elizabeth Allen, wife of William Allen, clerk of the parish of Clondroghet [Clondrohid], claimed he was deprived of 'his church living ...of Killemartra [and] Ballyvory [Ballyvourney].[7]

From an Inquisition of 1625 we learn that Donoghe Mac Carthy lived at Dromemonie [Dromonig] and also held Dromgarrie, Prohussbegg (at this time Prohus was divided into Prohusmore and -begg), Caherdaghine [Caherdaha], Clonetikertine [Cloontycarty] and Inishbrickane. He died in 1605. His son Dermod mortgaged Dromonig to another kinsman, Donogh McDermod of Towry [Tower] and Dromagarry to Patrick Sarsfield of Cork. Dues from these lands were paid to the Lord of Muskerry and also 13s. 4d. yearly to Fynine Mac Dermod Oge Mac Carthy of Dundareirke.

Nicholas Skiddy of Cork, held lands at Cahirdagh [Cahirdaha] and 'Cloontikeartin' also. About 1632 William Greatrix was enfoeffed of these lands. Greatrix also got Dromonig and Dromagarry. In 1688 Edmond Gould owned Dromonig, Dromagarry, Prohusbeg and Inchibrickane. Inchibrickane had earlier been mortgaged by Dermod mcDonogh to David Gould. The Gould family were Catholics of Norman extraction and are still associated with the parish.

Nicholas Skiddy seems to have had Candroma in 1632; he enfoeffed Greatrix, who in turn enfoeffed the Lord of Muskerry. Rahoonagh was mortgaged by Greatrix to the Lord of Muskerry and was afterwards given to James Baldwin. It is interesting to note that in the *Books of Survey and Distribution*, which record details of lands expropriated under the Acts of Settlement and Explanation (1663 and 1665) following the Cromwellian wars, this James Baldwin has a "w" after his name to symbolise 'Innocent Papist'. As the same symbol is given after the name of John Colthurst who received lands in Ballyvourney, we can put this down to scribal error.

This is the first coming of the Baldwin family to the parish, whom we shall treat of in more detail later. They were to be prominent landholders until the great land redistribution at the end of the 19th century.

The Civil Survey set itself to give 'The Description of the Meares & bounds of the Said Parish of Kilnamartyra, & of other things of note, or Eminency therein Consisting of fifteen Plowlands'.[8] The spelling of the English version of the parish name given here corresponds to the modern English spelling in common use, and is the first recorded instance of this format being used. Earlier and later versions offer many variations (as we have seen) – indeed the official spelling is still Kilnamartery, although this accords with neither the orthography of the Gaelic original nor local pronunciation of the English name.

The Survey continues:

> 'The generality of ye soil is cold, Mountainous, & Rocky, & not proper for much tillage. Here's a small Brook running thro' this parrish, call'd Sillane Beg. Timber woods there are some in this parrish... The tythes of this parish, is one Entire Rectory, here's ye Parochial Church of this parish Standing on the south side of the Castle of Dundaryrke...'[9]

The survey then proceeds to describe the townlands held by each proprietor: Dermott mc Dermott Carthy 'of Dundaryrk Irish papist' held 'Dunedaryrk', 'Rathleigh', 'both Breghanes' [indicating Brehaun split in two] and 'Dromreag'. The total is estimated at three ploughlands; this is further broken down as 620 acres of profitable land plus 100 unprofitable or waste; the value of the whole in 1641 is given as £50. 'On the p^{r}misses is a small Castle worth £100 wherein is kept a Garison, & a state [*recte* slate] quarry. There's a yeally [*sic, recte* yearly] Chief Rent of £6 with suit of Court Leet & Barron to ye Mannor of Macromp. Answerable out of ye p^{r}misses to ye L^d of Muskery, Irish papist.'[10]

A Court Leet (*Curia Purva*) was a manorial court which tried petty offenses. It predated justices of the peace. The Court Baron (*Curia Magna*) as the name suggest dealt with more weighty issues – including land tenure.[11]

The same individual held 'West Dromreage', 'Shanvallyshane', 'Keallfinchere' [Kylefinchin], 'low^r Ballyvige', Knockroe, 'Cloncolydeadh' [Cluain Chúil Uí Dheagh? name now unknown locally], and 'Aghachony' [Aghacunna], given as 802 profitable acres (including woodland worth £200) and 508 unprofitable. The 1641 valuation was £40. The Survey also notes a slate quarry here but doesn't specify where.

The later *Books of Survey and Distribution* give the proprietor of the above lands in 1641 as Daniell m[c] Dermod Carthy, rather than Dermott mcDermott. As we know that Daniel McDermod was head of Sliocht Thuath na Dromann in 1641 and held Dundareirke castle this latter is correct. The Civil Survey itself continues on to mention 'Dan[l] M[c]Derm[tt] afores[d]' as if this was the name given for the lands previously mentioned. This Daniel is then ascribed the lands of 'Knocksherme & Killnarowrog' [Knocksaharn and Kilmakaroge] with 125 profitable and 150 unprofitable acres, valued at £4.

The Lord of Muskerry, by mortgage from William Greatrix 'English Prot: deceas'd', held lands at 'South Cahirdah', 'Cule I-Readegane', 'Culeiverihy', 'Gortinemall' and 'Cloentybertine.' There was also a slate quarry here. Six hundred and sixty of the 720 acres were deemed profitable, including 340 acres of woodland with timber fit for building worth £100. The 1641 valuation of the whole was £50. The Survey notes that the mortgage was acknowledged by William's son Valentine. This was Valentine 'the Stroker', of whom we shall treat of in more detail later. Cule I-Readagane and Culeiverihy (presumably Cúil Uí Réadagáin and Cúil Uí Mhuirithe, respectively) are not known locally as placenames, but the Uí Mhuirithe or Murrays have been associated with the parish into modern times. Neither is Cloentybertine known, unless it be a corruption of Cloontycarty.

As all of the above mentioned lands held by the Lord of Muskerry on mortgage from Greatrix are described as being bounded on the east by Caherkereen and 'Upper Ballywoe', [Ballyvoig]; on the south by Knocksaharn and the river Toon; on the west by Dromleigh and Ballyvourney and by Caherdaha to the north, we can get an approximation of their location.

The Lord of Muskerry also held Upper Ballyvoig and Lisboy on a mortgage from 'Owen Finin Carthy dec[d.] Irish pap[t.]' This

Owen was a brother of Daniel Mac Fynyne mac Donnell Oge of Dundareirke. We know that this Daniel pre-deceased his father Finghín, who died in 1637. The Daniel McDermott who held Dundareirke plus other lands in 1641 was the grandson of Daniel who died before his father in 1637. Dermot, son to Daniel and nephew of Owen died in 1638, aged 20.[12] Such a mortality rate across three generations in only three to four years perhaps indicates internecine strife over the leadership of Sliocht Thuath na Dromann in the unsettled period of the Elizabethan wars. Alternatively, as the Dermitius Mac Dowell Oge killed as a rebel in 1601 is almost certainly correctly named Dermot Mac Donell Oge (as Dubhgall was not a name used by the MacCarthy) and therefore brother of Finghin, it may show heavy involvement by the MacCarthys of Dundareirke in the rebellion.

Teige Mac Dermott oge Carthy, termed deceased Irish Papist of 'Caherkearine', held 110 profitable and 10 unprofitable acres in Caherkereen. The survey also notes 'On the p^{r}misses is ye Walls of a ruin'd house...'[13] This must be the mansion mentioned earlier of which only the 'Simné' now stands. It may have been destroyed in the 1641 Rebellion; perhaps destroyed by Teige who was possibly later killed himself by the Cromwellians. This Teige also held 360 acres at Dromleigh, 'Dirryfinine' [Derryfineen] and 'Gortnabemy', [Gortnabinne]. This Dromleigh, also mentioned earlier, was probably in Ballyvourney, bordering Cill na Martra and is not the Dromleigh in Kilmichael. This same parcel of land is also listed in the *Deeds, Leases, Mortgages, And Marriage Settlements Baronies of Muskerry East and Muskerry West, County of Cork 1708-1773*. We read that the Governor and Company for making Hollow Sword Blades in England sold to Humphry Massy 'of Macromp ...in consideration of 5 lbs. in lease and 176 lbs. 13 s. 3 d. the town and lands of Drumleagh, Derryfinin, Gortnebriny [Gortnabinna], Cahirkerin situated in B[arony] of Muskerry and Co. of Corke and were late part of estate of

Donogh, *late Earl of Clancarthy,* attainted of treason, yearly rent of 28 lbs.' This document was sworn in June 1713. The same source also records that in September 1714 Thos. Sheares of Cork sold to Francis Gray, a merchant in Cork, the lands of 'Canndrommy', 'Cleneykerteene' [Cloontycarty], Knocksaharn and 'Kilmacarronvroge' [Kilmakaroge] for £1,344. This Thomas was possibly an ancestor of the Sheares brothers, leaders of the Cork United Irishmen.

The Civil Survey laid out 4,070 acres of forfeited land, of which 2,567 acres was deemed to be profitable. The 1641 valuation for the land of Cill na Martra was given as £206, quite a considerable sum in those days.

To this may be added Coolavokig, held by the Lord of Muskerry and treated by the Civil Survey as part of the civil parish of Ballyvourney. Of the 500 acres here, 300 were deemed to be unprofitable, including 180 acres of timber wood for building valued at £300. The 1641 valuation of Coolavokig is assessed at £10. A good indication of the state or the area post-1641 is given by the remark that:

'The Nature of ye Soil is Cold, & Craggy, & if manur'd with dung (as it was when inhabited) indifferent good for tillage, of Course, lying at present Wholly Waste'.[14]

This echoes the description of the Rectory of Macroom given in 1591 as "Est locus vastatus", meaning the place was devastated.

The Lord of Muskerry, as we have seen, also held 'Rathanagh' (Rahoonagh) by mortgage from William Greatrix. Of its 200 acres, 100 was deemed to be profitable, including 60 acres of timber. The value in 1641 is given as £3 10s. Candroma was also held by Lord Muskerry on a mortgage from Greatrix. Only 80 of its 200 acres were deemed profitable, with a valuation of £8. The surveyors noted 'The Nature of ye Soil is Rocky, is indiff^t good for tillage being now Waste'.[15]

The Survey records Nicholas Skiddy, 'Irish Papist of Corke', as holding Prohus Mor and Beg (this division is no longer extant) along with Dromouny [Dromonig], which also appears to incorporate Dromagarry.[16]

It is to be noted that when laying out the bounds of 'Ballyvourny Parish' the Civil Survey says that 'on the South the s^d Parish Extendeth to the lands of Lack, in the Parish of Kilanamartra…'[17], yet in treating of Cill na Martra Leac is not mentioned at all. The place can hardly have been overlooked by the surveyors, therefore it must be that Leac and other modern townland names not mentioned must be included in the townlands mentioned; or else they were already held by colonial settlers and therefore not for expropriation. That fact, along with placenames no longer extant, help to account for discrepancies in acreage between the Civil Survey and the later Ordnance Survey of the 19th century. Thus Butler writes of 'Dirragh, the modern Derragh, apparently with Lackbeg and Lackmore' and Kilmakaroge 'probably included the modern Gortanadan also.'[18]

It is also to be noted that by 1641 only two members of Sliocht Thuath na Dromann were proprietors of land in Cill na Martra. We have seen earlier how both Sir Cormac McTeig and Cormac mc Dermod, as Lords of Muskerry, had attempted to grab the clan lands for themselves. By 1641 this had obviously been successful.

At the Restoration of the monarchy in England in 1660, the Lord of Muskerry, who was then the Earl of Clancarthy, got his estates back. The fact that his wife was the sister to the influential Marquis of Ormond was of some significance here. His followers, however, did not. We learn from Butler[19] that many of his followers had been reluctant to rise out as they had foreseen just such a scenario arising. Donough McCarthy, the then 2nd Viscount Muskerry and Earl of Clancarthy, had promised them he would accept no outcome for himself that did not include his followers.

A further pressure on the native landholders at the Restoration came from the fact that the Act of Settlement contained a clause forbidding Catholics to be restored to properties in corporate towns. In Co. Cork, they were instead to be compensated with other lands in the baronies of Barrymore and Muskerry. As nearly all of Barrymore was hold by the Earl of Barrymore, a Protestant whose lands were never confiscated, the nett effect was to leave the lands of Muskerry as sole means of compensation to the townspeople who could not get possession of their former properties.

However, other clauses in the Act of Settlement also specified that confiscated lands in Muskerry which had not been given to Cromwellian adventurers or hadn't been restored to their orginal proprietors, should be granted to Charles MacCarthy (son of Donogh, Earl of Clancarthy), Viscount Muskerry. But this Charles had been killed in 1665, ironically fighting for the English against the Dutch in a battle at sea, so their lands were now to go to Charles' son and heir, Charles James.

A further clause gave the Earl of Clancarthy, grandfather of the infant Charles James, the right to leave or grant lands to the former proprietors. In the event of Donogh's death, his wife would have this right. Donogh died also in 1665 and his widow used the relevant clause to restore the former owners to their lands on long leases at nominal rents. 'In this way the Mac Carthys...of Kilnamartyra... recovered their former estates.' [20]

Their tenure was to be short-lived, however, as the Earl of Clancarthy and his followers took the Jacobite side after the Williamite coup of 1688. They again rose out in rebellion. Thus W. Maziere Brady records that Richard Brown was Protestant rector of Macroom and Ballyvourney in 1669. He also held the living of 'Kilnamartery' from 1685-1706. He was recorded as being a 'sufferer in rebellion' in 1688. On 20 December 1689 his uncle Richard Parr, vicar of Camberwell, London, wrote to the Archbishop of Canterbury on behalf of 'his nephew, Richard Browne, an outcast clergyman from Ireland'.

With the defeat of King James in 1690, Clancarthy and almost all his followers finally lost their lands in the Williamite confiscations.

A list of persons outlawed in Cork in 1690 includes 'Charles M'Carthey' of 'Tonadromah, esq.' Callaghan M'Carthy, "Gent, Toughmadromin' is on a list of those outlawed for foreign treason in Co. Cork, 1691-98.[21]

According to the *Books of Postings and Sales*, Charles MacCarthy of 'Toonadromin' forfeited Dundareirke, along with 'Rathleag' [Raleigh], Curragheen, Brehanes, Dromreagh, Shanwallyshane and Keelfunchin [Kylefinchin].

Thus ended Sliocht Thuath na Dromann.

In a final historical irony the MacCarthys, who had always followed the crown in order to retain their lands, finally lost them by being followers of King James.

Valentine 'the Stroker'

Given the origins of the name Cill na Martra, it is perhaps appropriate that the parish has at least some association with the international healing sensation of the 17th century, Valentine Greatrakes (also spelt Greatraks, Greatrix or Greatorix)

Valentine Greatrakes was born on 14 February 1628, (hence the Christian name), at Affane castle, near Dungarvan, Co. Waterford. He was the son of William Greakrakes and Mary Harris, daughter of Sir Edward Harris, Chief Justice for Munster. Valentine's grandfather, also William, was from the village of Great Rakes in Derbyshire, England, from where the family took its surname. The Rev. Samuel Hayman's history of the family[22] (written in 1863) tells us that the name signifies a large cleft or fissure in a rock. This William of Derbyshire was born in c. 1540 and came to Ireland as a soldier at the time of the Munster rebellion. He became a planter at Affane, on the Blackwater. Smith's *History of Waterford* (1773) mentions the castle of Norrisland at new Affane, 'built by one Greatrakes' saying it was remarkable for large orchards. Smith credits Greatrakes with the introduction of cider to Ireland.

At the outbreak of the 1641 rebellion, the family fled to England. In 1647 Valentine returned to Ireland and with the coming of Cromwell's army he became an officer in the Earl of Orrery's regiment.

With the defeat of the Irish, Greatrakes left the army and took posession of the lands at Affane. He was also given public office as a reward for his military service, being appointed Clerk for the Peace for County Cork, Registrar of Transplantation, and Justice of the Peace. In 1661, he was involved in the trial for witchcraft of Florence Newton of Youghal. Greatrakes and the officials subjected her to 'trial by ordeal' to show she was a witch.

In 1666, at the height of his fame Greatrakes wrote an autobiography, entitled *A Brief Account of Mr Valentine Greatrak's and divers of the Strange Cures by him lately performed. Written by himself in a Letter, addressed to the Honourable Robert Boyle, Esq. Whereinto are annexed the Testimonials of several Eminent and Worthy persons of the chief matter of fact, therein related.*
Boyle was one of the most famous men of his day, and also of Munster planter stock.

In his book Greatrakes states that in 1663, at the aga of 34, he 'had an impulse or strange persuasion' which convinced him 'there was bestowed on me a gift of curing the King's Evil', (Charles II suffered from the skin disease scrofula).

He cured a local youth, William Maher of Salterbridge, Cappoquin, of scrofula, and his fame quickly spread. Soon the crowds attending his residence were so large he was forced to relocate to Youghal. The crowds continued to grow as did the list of ailments cured. Boatloads of people from England looking for cures began to arrive.

The Dublin newspaper *The Intelligencer* through the summer of 1665 has many accounts of his deeds, including 'above threescore cured by him in one night, of deafness, blindness, cancers, sciatieas, palsies, impostumes, fistulas, and the like...'[23]

Greatrakes ministered to the sick by rubbing the affected parts, hence the sobriquet 'The Stroker'. It is recorded that he accepted no money in return.

In January 1665 the English aristocrat Lord Conway urged the Archbishop of Dublin to persuade a reluctant Geatrakes to travel to England to treat his wife. This is the only known occasion he demanded payment; he received £155 to cover expenses and compensate for 'the hazards of the enraged seas'. He failed to cure Lady Conway but stayed on for a month and reputedly cured many. Charles II invited him to London where many more flocked to see him.

By the time of his death in Affane in 1683, he owned land in Waterford and Tipperary as well as in England. In 1678, he sold his lands at Clohina to Colonel James Baldwin. In 1683, Baldwin willed this land to his nephew Herbert.

Valentine Geatrakes has left us a mention of his lands at Clohina among his papers: 'Amongst the manuscripts in the British Museum is one bearing the press mark, "Additional 25692" and endorsed "Accounts of Valentine Greatrakes of Affane, Co Waterford, 1663-1679"'. [24]

The Account book contains 57 foolscap leaves. Under the heading 'August 2^d 1667', it records:

> 'An account of w^{ht} moneys I received of Dermond Mc Carthy out of my estate in Musgry for ye years 56 & 57.[25]

On 16 November 1667 he received £5 1s. 9d. from Derby McCarthy. It also shows sums of money owed to him for 'workeinge' 2,000 barrel and hogshead staves and 200 'Dozen of

Hoopes', showing he was exploiting the woodlands of Clohina for coopering. By 8 June 1688, McCarthy still owed him 'ye sum of' £4 18s. 9d.

On 4 August 1670 'Derby McCarthy brought out of Musgery ye day and yeare above' 2,400 or 54 horse loads of Ferkin staves along with 48 dozen 'of Hoopes', or four horse loads. Derby McCarthy was given £1 to pay the carriers. An entry for 8 November 1671 gives an account of 'casks and other things' in Affane 'in ye cyder house.' This suggests Greatrakes was using woodlands at Clohina to provide barrels for the cider being produced in Affane.

Valentine "The Stroker" still commands interest in modern times. In 2001 the Abbey Theatre ran a play about him entitled *Blackwater Angel*. He has also been the subject of a short article in the January/February 2007 edition of *History Ireland*.[26]

In another confluence of history, Valentine's brother John had a daughter Magdalene Greatrakes. Her son, John Gwyn of Cork, married Catherine the sister of Sir James Cotter of Ballinsperig whom we shall mention later in connection with Art Ó Laoghaire.

Valentine's only sister, Mary, married John Nettles of Waterford, part of the Herefordshire family which come to Ireland as planters in 1639 and from whom Nettleville near Macroom also took its name.

The Baldwins

In an article in the *Southern Star* in 1970,[27] C.J.F. McCarthy held that the Baldwins probably first came to Co. Cork in Elizabethan times. By the early 17th century there were two branches of the family near Bandon. The first of them to come to Cill na Martra was James Baldwin, who held some lands in Ballyvoig. In 1678, as we have seen, he purchased lands in Clohina from Valentine Greatrakes; his will, dated 1683, refers to 'the lands of Clogheena which I lately purchased of Valentine Geatrakes'. Baldwin copperfastened his tenure of the land by getting a crown grant in 1686 of Rahoona, Clohina and Gortanimall, some 1,939 acres. On James' death his nephew Walter got Ballyvoig and another nephew Herbert got Clohina and adjacent lands. These were sons of James' brother, also Herbert, and Mary Newce from whose family Newcestown is named.

Usually taken as being of English origin, the name originated in Germany. It occurs in documents relating to Ireland from the 13th century onwards. Numerous instances of the name (and its synonyms Baldon and Baldin – in Cill na Martra they were known in Irish as na Báildingí) are recorded in the Justiciary Rolls and Fiants, especially in relation to the southeast. The 'census' of 1659 shows it figuring prominently in Co. Waterford. The Baldwins were originally from Shropshire on the English-Welsh border.[28] They had family connections with the Herberts, Welsh aristocrats and through them with Ann Parr, sister of Catherine Parr, last wife of Henry VIII. By an irony of history, Mary O'Connell was married off to James Baldwin of Clohina because she wanted to marry a Mr. Herbert from Wales who had been shipwrecked off Iveragh. This Herbert turned out to be a distant cousin of Baldwin. The Herberts of Powys were the senior branch of the family which included the Herberts of Muckross in Killarney.[29] Local lore has it that Mary O'Connell often chided her husband by remarking 'Remember, only for you Mr. Baldwin, I should now be Countess of Powys!' Thus the name Herbert was passed on as a Christian name through different generations of Baldwins.

Mary and James Baldwin also had a son Herbert who became a doctor like his father and served in the British Army during the Napoleonic Wars. He and his brother Walter who lived at the house in Clohina often quarrelled. In 1802 Herbert set the house on fire in a fit of temper. In 1810 the family reloacated to

Gortanimill having built a big house there.

This Herbert was MP for Cork city from 1832-1837. The end of Dr Baldwin's political career came in a controversial fashion. He had lost the election of 1835 but 'regained his seat on petition'.[30] On 3 May 1837 a meeting was called in the County Courthouse in Cork. The topic of the meeting was the county representation in Parliament. Baldwin was a Liberal supporter and his fellow Liberal Fergus O' Connor of Connorville had, in a mirror image of Baldwin, first been elected in 1835 and then unseated on petition from Richard Longfield of Longueville, a Tory, who was then deemed elected. This gives a flavour of the political in-fighting of the time. At that time the franchise was confined to owners of freehold of £10 or above. This had been introduced with the Catholic Emancipation Act of 1829 to reduce the Catholic vote.

The meeting on 3 May became rancorous with disagreement as to who should be credited with Emancipation. Baldwin downplayed the role of Daniel O'Connell, his own first cousin, and gave the credit to Robert Peel and the Duke of Wellington.

Redmond O'Driscoll, editor of *The Southern Reporter*, wrote an account of the meeting in the paper which incensed Baldwin. A few days later, O'Driscoll was walking along Grand Parade, accompanied by Fr. William O'Sullivan and Joseph Hayes, a prominent businessman, when Baldwin confronted him. The angry Baldwin called O'Driscoll 'a blackguard false reporter'. In line with the etiquette of the time, O'Driscoll sent a friend named Henry Burke to call on Baldwin for an explanation. Baldwin admitted the remark and Burke challenged him to a duel with O'Driscoll. Baldwin, however, sent an emissary to O'Driscoll to decline the challenge. O'Driscoll published a full account in his paper and accused Baldwin of being 'a bully, a braggart, a liar and a coward'.

Baldwin issued a statement denying that he had never called

O'Driscoll a false reporter. Instead, he said O'Driscoll had misheard a comment he was making to a friend of his complaining about 'a blackguard false report'. Baldwin's political career came to an end later that year, when he resigned his seat.[31]

His brother Connell J. Baldwin was evidently made of sterner stuff. Having been educated by the Jesuits in France, he joined the navy at 14. He later joined the army and fought in the Napoleonic wars. In 1826 he raised a regiment to serve under the Emperor of Brazil. Like his brother, he became involved in politics on finally settling in Canada, where he died in 1861.

Dr. Baldwin had also died earlier that same year. The Cork Examiner of 18 January 1861 records:

> 'Death of Dr Baldwin, JP,- At his residence, Clohina, on the 17th inst. Herbert Baldwin M.D., J.P., after having attained the fine old age of seventy-nine years and a half.'

It is noticeable that they were still known as the Baldwins of Clohina, even though then resident in Gortanimill. Gortanimill, in fact, was the archtypal 'Big House' of the time. Baldwin kept 22 racehorses, three stallions and hounds. When he died he was £34,000 in debt. His daughter married John O'Sullivan of Beara, a relative of O'Sullivan Beare. His son, also Herbert, died without issue. Mary Ann and John O'Sullivan had one son, Herbert Baldwin O'Sullivan. In 1888 he married into the Hennessey family, of brandy fame.

The family finally left the parish in 1891 as the Land Acts began undoing the confiscations of previous centuries.

Art Ó Laoghaire

When Mary O'Connell, aunt of Daniel O'Connell, the Liberator, married James Baldwin of Clohina, he was almost unique among the new landlord class in having become Catholic. The O'Connells of Derrynane formed part of a small remnant of Gaelic, Catholic, wealthy landowners who had managed to survive the vicissitudes of history. They tended to be located in upland or peninsular regions away from the eyes of the authorities. In Munster they included such families as the Hennesseys and Nagles of north Co. Cork and the O'Donoughues of Glenflesk, as well as the O'Connells. This mountainous spine of the old culture tended to intermarry, and given the small number of families involved, it would be natural for Catholic landowners of planter stock to be viewed as potential marriage partners; marriage, then of course, being primarily a means of passing property through the generations.

Thus it was that Mary married James Baldwin of Clohina while her sister Eileen was married at 15 years of age to an elderly landowner named O'Connor, in Firies, Co. Kerry, in or around 1758. Eileen or Eibhlín Dhubh Ní Chonaill as she would be known in history, was widowed after 6 months. In 1767 Eibhlín Dhubh came to visit her sister Mary. While both were on a trip to Macroom, through the window of a house in the Square, Eibhlín Dhubh saw Art Ó Laoghaire in the street and as the opening line of her famous *Caoineadh* relates:

> *'Mo ghrá go daingean tú*
> *Lá dá bhfaca thú'*

Despite the disapproval of her family Eibhlín and Art were married. The newspaper of 19 December 1767 carried notice of the marriage of Mr. Arthur O'Leary 'to the Widow Connor of Iveragh'. The couple went to live in Art's house in Raleigh.

Though still in his early twenties, Art had recently returned from the Continent where he had been a captain of Hussars in the Austro-Hungarian army.

This was the era of the Penal Laws and the 'Hidden Ireland'. The O'Connells and their fellow Gaelic Catholic landowners' got by with a policy of not drawing attention to themselves. This is illustrated by an anecdote contained in *The Last Colonel of the Irish Brigade*, by Mrs M.J. O'Connell (a collection of letters, etc., dealing with the history of the O'Connell family) about a traveller from Cork who was given generous hospitality in Derrynane. When he mentioned to his hosts that as thanks he would give a glowing account of them in a book he intended to write, he was promptly shown the door.

Due to the fact the he had been living abroad as an army officer and also the fact of his own proud personality, Art had none of this 'ceann fé' which natives of all classes had to adopt at home. The *Caoineadh* describes his apparel:

> '*Gur bhreá thíodh hata dhuit*
> *Faoi bhanda óir tarraingthe,*
> *Claíomh cinn airgid*
> ....
> *Is each caol ceanann fút*
> ....
> *Is maith thíodh biorán duit*
> *Daingean faoi cháimbric*
> *Is hata faoi lása*
> *Tar éis teacht duit thar sáile*'

The picture given here of Art, dressed in imported finery, riding a fine horse and wearing a silver-handled sword was guaranteed to infuriate the authorities. The bearing of arms by Catholics was itself illegal under the Penal Laws

Art was unfortunate that his new neighbour was Abraham

Morris, Sheriff of Cork, who resided at Hanover Hall near Macroom. It was not long before the two were bitter enemies.

The story of Art's death is well known, but its precise details are anything but. On 15 August 1771, Art placed a notice in the *Cork Evening Post* that he was prepared to stand trial at the next assizes in Cork for unspecified crimes he had been charged with by 'different persons'. On 7 December Morris gave public notice in the *Cork Evening Post*, that he has put £20 reward for the capture of Art, 'a fellow of a character most notoriously infamous'. He charged Art with trying to kill him at Hanover Hall, wounding one of his servants and stealing a gun. Shortly afterwards, the Muskerry Constitutional Society, a planter cabal, put 20 guineas on Art's head, calling him an outlaw on his keeping.

On 19 December Art responded with a long newspaper notice giving his side. He stated he had visited Hanover Hall on 13 July 1771 to discuss some legal matters with Morris. He claimed Morris had abused him and as Art left for home the High Sheriff and one of his servants, both armed, followed him. They fired at Art, wounding him. Art claimed he had then wrested the gun from the servant in self-defence. He had later given the weapon to a Justice of the Peace along with a complaint about the attack on him. The notice is signed Arthur Leary and is given as 'Dated at Rathleigh, October 19, 1771', showing Art was still residing at home.

James Baldwin was a Justice of the Peace and it is most likely to him at Clohina that Art gave the gun and made his complaint. All of the other Justices of the Peace in the district would most likely have tried to arrest him. Baldwin, however, was apparently always worried about his tenure of his own lands since he became a Catholic and was unlikely to do anything to help Art despite the family connection. He is remembered in history and folklore as 'an fear caol spágach'. Baldwin's own interests of course would have been with the landed classes. The *Hibernian Chronicle* of 7

May 1772 carried a notice that two horses had been stolen on the night of 28 April 'from the lands of Clohinagh near Macroom', the horses being owned by James Baldwin. A reward of two guineas for the horse or four guineas for the horse and thief was offered. The notice continues that one John Mahony, dairyman to Baldwin, was the suspect. He ran away the same night and his wife was quoted as saying: "twas he who stole them; he's a tall, lusty man, and slightly marked with the Small-pox'.

Sean Ó Tuama quotes folklore collector Proinsias Ó Ceallaigh of Baile Bhúirne who collected a local tradition that jealousy was at the base of Morris' hatred of Art:

> 'Do bhuail seanduine umam i Magh Chromtha … agus duirt sé liom gur éad a thosnaigh an t-easaontas idir é féin agus Morris…go raibh rince i dtigh Mhorris oíche éigin agus go raibh Art ag an rince; go raibh cailín anabhreá ag an rince, cailín go raibh Morris go mór léi; gur tháinig Art taobh istigh de an oíche sin agus gur thainig éad buile ar Mhorris'.[32]

This tallies with a variation of the text of the *Caoineadh* which runs:

> *'Mo chara is mo rún tú*
> *Ní raibh le casadh sa gcúirt leat*
> *Ach go rabhais ciontach*
> *I bpeaca na drúise,*
> *Agus ní tusa ba chiontach*
> *Ach an bhuín do bhí umhal duit.'*[33]

Ó Tuama's judgement is that: 'i bhfianise na línte thuas is féidir bheith cuíosach deimhnitheach gur labhair an seanchas fíor.'[34]

At any rate, the die was cast and the authorities were determined to put down the upstart. Things seem to have come to a head at a horse race at Dunisky near Macroom, where Art's chestnut mare beat Morris' horse. A variant telling is that Art 'took the brush' at a meeting of the Muskerry Hunt.[35] Morris immediately invoked a little used statute from the time of William III which stated no Catholic could own a horse worth more than £5 and also that any offer to a Catholic of £5 for a horse must be accepted. It is sometimes objected that the Penal Laws were more or less in abeyance by this time; while not formally rescinded they had fallen into disuse. That this is untrue is shown by a land grab in Shanballyshane in 1762. A 'Protestant Discoverer' named John Forster of Dublin, a bridlecutter, advertised in the *Cork Evening Post* that he had 'discovered' that certain lands in Shanballyshane were owned by a Catholic. Under the terms of the Penal Laws he now laid legal claim to these lands. Another proof is that Richard Hedges of Macroom castle reported on 16 October 1712 that after a search over a number of days he had arrested the Parish Priest Donogh Sweeney 'A Doctor of the Sorbonne' and sent him to Cork Gaol for refusing to take the Oath of Abjuration.[36]

As Morris would have intended, Art was outraged by the offer and refused. The two may have come to blows. Art was immediatly proclaimed an outlaw. There is uncertainty about what happened next. There is an enigmatic reference in a letter written by Colonel Daniel O'Connell of the Irish Brigade (who was in Ireland on a recruiting mission in 1773) on 15 April from a relative's house in Clonakilty to his brother Maurice (Muiris a'Chaipín) in Derrynane saying 'I am glad to hear our friend Arthur has arrived safely'. It is believed by some that the O'Connells helped Art to leave the area – perhaps to Kerry; perhaps abroad on one of their smuggling trips to the Continent. Another tradition says Art stayed at home and tells of Eibhlín loading the guns while Art held off a siege at his house in Raleigh. What we do know is that on 4 May 1773, Art prepared to leave his home at Raleigh. Some portent of doom caused him to turn back at the gate to say a last farewell to his wife and children.

> *'Nuair ghabhais amach an geata*
> *D'fhillis ar ais go tapaidh,*
> *Do phógais do dhís leanbh,*
> *Do phógais mise ar bharra baise.*
> *Dúrais, 'A Eibhlín, éirigh id sheasamh*
> *Agus cuir do ghnó chun taisce*
> *Go luaimneach is go tapaidh.*
> *Táimse ag fágáil an bhaile*
> *Is ní móide go deo go gcasfainn'.*
> *Níor dheineas dá chaint ach magadh,*
> *Mar bhíodh á rá liom go minic cheana.'*

The last two lines hint at the tension he had been feeling since being on the run as a proclaimed outlaw.

Art headed northwards, apparently intending to ambush Morris, who was visiting Drishane castle, on his return home towards Macroom. At Carraig an Ime, Art called at a tavern owned by Cornelius Duggan. He bought rum for everybody and outlined what he intended to do. An informer, named in the *Caoineadh* as Seán MacUaithne, got word to Morris who promptly sent for the military. The military caught up with Art somewhere beyond Carraig an Ime.

Art retreated before the soldiers; local tradition says he mocked them by keeping just out of range as they fired at him. Arriving back at Carraig an Ime, Art crossed the river while the soldiers took up position at a pound in the village. One shot, supposed to have been fired by a one-eyed marksman, hit Art in the neck or side. The spot where he fell would suggest he was out of range of a musket ball and was hit by a fluke. However, another theory[37] is that Art remained on his horse for a hundred yards or so after he was hit, before falling from the saddle. This spot in the townland of Carrigonirtane is marked by a monument today. Pádraig Ó Maidín quotes the soldier who fired the fatal shot as telling the officer in charge 'I have covered the buckle of his shoe and will hit him in the side'. Folklore has it the the soldiers returned to Macroom to be rewarded at a 'grog shop' beside the Latin school near the bridge (the same school an t-Athair Peadar attended as a boy and wrote of in *Mo Scéal Féin).*

Art's body was left where it fell. His horse returned to Raleigh where, as the *Caoineadh* recounts:

> '*Is níor chreideas riamh dod mharbh*
> *gur thánig chugham do chapall*
> *Is a srianta léi go talamh,*
> *Is fuil do chroí ar a leacain*
> *Síar go t'iallait ghreanta*
> ....
> *Thugas léim go táirsigh*
> *An dara léim go geata*
> *An triú léim ar do chapall.*'

The fact that so much of Art's blood was on the mare from the head to the saddle, would support the theory that Art, mortally wounded and bleeding profusely, stayed on the horse's back for some short period after being shot.

The horse brought Eibhlín to the spot where Art lay, having bled to death:

> '*Do chuid fola leat* ' *na sraithibh;*

*Is níor fhanas le hí ghlanadh
Ach í ól suas lem basaibh.*'

Here and over the next day or so of the wake and funeral Eibhlín Dhubh composed the *Caoineadh Airt Uí Laoghaire*, one of the finest existing examples of Gaelic literature. Art's body was removed to his home at Raleigh for waking and was buried in the nearby graveyard of Dundareirke. As the epic puts it:

'*Is nuair thiocfaidh chugham abhaile
Conchubar beag an cheana
Is Fear Ó Laoghaire an leanbh
Fiafróid díom go tapaidh
Cár fhágas féin a n-athair.
Neosad dóibh faoi mhairg
Gur fhágas i gCill na Martar.
Glaofaid siad ar a n-athair,
Is ní bheidh sé acu le freagairt.*'

As the final piece of vindictiveness, the authorities would not allow his remains to be buried in consecrated ground but in the field adjacent to the graveyard

Eagle presented to Art Ó Laoghaire by the Empress of Austria

At that time, Dundareirke and other ancient graveyards were the property of the Established Church. Catholics had to request permission for burial and no Catholic rites were to be carried out (hence the tradition of the prayers being said at Lúibín na gCorp). Art's body lay there for some time (until the following October by some accounts; for a few years by others – though the shorter period seems the more likely) before it was removed for burial at Kilcrea Friary. His grave is marked by the lines:

'Lo! Arthur O'Leary, generous, handsome, brave
Slain in his bloom, lies in this humble grave-'

He was 26 years old when he was killed.

It has sometimes been suggested that the *Caoineadh* was composed by a professional *'bean chaointe'*. However, there is no reason to believe that the bulk of it (some verses are ascribed to Art's father and sister) was not composed by Eibhlín Dhubh herself. Her mother Maire Ní Dhonnchada (of the O'Donoghues of

Glenflesk, patrons of Aogán Ó Rathaille)- also known as Máire Ní Duibh- was herself a poet. Young as she was when she was first widowed at Firies, Eibhlín composed a caoineadh for her late husband. Ó Tuama tells us 'mhair fo-líne as ag daoine i nDoire Fhionáin, a h-áit dhúchais, go ceann i bhfad.'[38]

Eibhlín was raised in the last remnants of Gaelic minor aristocracy. As Rachel Bromwich puts it: 'she received her education entirely from the rich culture of her own race ... she would have been familiar living in such a time and place, with the unexpected and violent deaths of those who had been a part of her ancestral surroundings. As she grew up, she would have assisted at wakes; and from them she would have formed certain ideas of the proper ceremonial accompanient to death ... The art of keening was one which was highly developed amd which had an ancient tradition behind it ...it is clear that the custom of keening for the dead belonged peculiarly to women.'[39]

Bromwich shows that Eibhlín Dhubh's *Caoineadh* fits firmly into the *caoineadh* tradition of Munster. Among the common motifs are:

- The Caoineadh is a direct address to the corpse, usually given in its presence.
- The opening line of each verse is a term of endearment
- Women mourn the hero's death
- There is a cursing of the hero's enemies, including his betrayer
- An enumeration of the hero's lineage

While the *caoineadh* is well attested and the professional '*bean chaointe*'was a respected figure, Bromwich finds it 'significant that it is the keens of true grief, uttered by the wife or mother or nurse of the dead man, whose merit has caused them to be handed down. Thus the *Keen for Art O'Leary* is the climax of a long traditon of keening, developed to a particulary fine art in this south western district of Munster.[40] She notes a close parallel between Eibhlín's work and the keen for Sir James Cotter who was hanged in 1720.

Bromwich also locates Eibhlín Dhubh's work within the wider Gaelic literature by noting similarities with 17th century Scots Gaelic poets Dorothy Brown (Diorbhail Nic A Bhriuthainn) and Mary McLeod. In paricular she notes that the image used by Mary McLeod in a lament for a McLeod chieftain.

'Chaill mi iuchair mo chùil'

is exactly parellelled by Eibhlín Dhubh:

*'Mar a bheadh glas a bheadh as thrúnc
's go raghadh an eochair amú'*.

Bromwich concludes that it 'is clear that both Eileen Dubh Ní Chonaill and Mary McLeod inherited a common traditon of keening...'[41] Indeed, as she also notes, the image of Eibhlín drinking Art's blood, previously quoted, ties the *Caoineadh* into the earliest Irish literary traditions Two examples are Deirdre mourning the death of Naoise: *'Agus do ghaibh ag pógadh Naoise agus ag ól a fola'* and Emer mourning Cuchulainn: *'do ghabh ag súgad a beól ₇ ac ól a fola...'*[42]

In an address given to the 3rd O'Leary clan gathering in Inchigeelagh on 13 September 1998, Peter O'Leary[43] notes that some scholars have seen similarities between Art's death in 1773 and that of other prominent Catholics earlier in the century. Ó Buachalla concedes a 'supeficial resemblance'[44] with the killings of Murty Og O'Sullivan (1754) and James Cotter (1720). Peter

O'Leary sees it as part of an ongoing anti-Catholic campaign by an extreme group centred in Co. Cork and led in Parliament by the Earl of Shannon. Further aspects of this campaign were pressuring the Hennesseys to leave north Cork (and find brandy fame and fortune in France) and making the Nagles conform to the Established Church.

The Cotter case is perhaps closest to Art's. Séamas Óg Mac Coitir was the son of Sir James Cotter, 'one of Ireland's most prominent Royalists who had served the Stuarts diligently.'[45] Sir James commanded Jacobite forces in Cork during the Williamite wars, but had been able to retain his lands in East Cork, centred on Ballinsperrig, Carrigtwohill, under the Treaty of Limerick. The famous Irish text *Párliament na mBan* was written for his son Séamas Óg by his tutor Fr. Ó Colmáin in 1697. This James Cotter (Séamas Óg) was hanged in Cork on 7 May 1720, having been convicted of sexually assaulting a Quaker named Elizabeth Squibb. However, it was widely believed this charge was just a pretext by a local Protestant Ascendancy faction who resented his politics and his brash (to them) behaviour of wearing a sword, and being an accomplished horseman. The judge who tried and sentenced him was his neighbour Sir St. John Broderick, son of Viscount Midleton. Broderick was an anti-Catholic bigot who was also reputedly jealous of Cotter as his wife had told him to ensure Cotter's acquittal. The parallels with Morris and Art Ó Laoghaire are striking.[46]

Clergy and Chapel
The new regime post-1690 moved quietly to flex its power. In 1703 the Irish Parliament passed an 'Act for Registering of Popish Clergy'. This act compelled every priest then in Ireland to register his name and certain other details, including the name of the 'Parishes of which they pretend to be Parish Priests' at the next Quarter sessions held after the feast of St. John the Baptist

in 1704. Each priest was also to get two people to enter recognizances on his behalf to the then huge amount of £50 each to ensure his good behaviour.

Records for the parish of Cill na Martra for the period from the mid-17th to mid- 18th centuries are not plentiful so this Act has fortuitously provided us with information. As the Penal Laws (2 Anne, cap. 7) forbade any parish priest to have a curate, we can assume there was only one priest for the parish.

The list for Co. Cork was registered at the General Sessions of the Peace for the County of Cork, held on 11 July 1704; 54 names altogether were registered for Co. Cork, excluding Cork city. The sixth on the list is that of Dermod Croneen, 36 years of age, Parish Priest of 'Ballyvorny and Kilnamartery'. He resided at Ballymakerry (Ballymakeera). He had been ordained in 1691 at Sayntus in France by Wil. Santomensis, Bishop of Sayntus. This was probably the ancient French diocese of Saintes which was in existence form the 3rd century up until 1801 when it was suppressed and its territory divided between the modern dioceses of Angouleme, La Rochelle and Poitiers. The modern city of Saintes is in the Charente Maritime province of France today. Dermot Carthy of Coorelegh (civil parish of Inchigeelagh) and John Callanan of Castletown each pledged £50 on his behalf.[47] The only Castletown in Cloyne diocese is Castletownroche; but as Callanan is a west Cork name either Castletownkinneigh or Castletownbere is probably meant here, with the closer one being the more likely.

Local parish records list the first priest resident in the parish as Daniel Riordan in 1752. We know he was still there in 1766 as an extract from the 'Returns of the State of Popery' ordered by the Irish Parliament from all Church of Ireland ministers as regards their parishes, states: 'Kilnamartery Reputed Popish priest resident in the parish of Kilnamartry, Daniel Riordan, March 27 1766'. An earlier account of 6 November 1731, states

'Kilnamartrya – no Masshouse, one reputed Popish Priest, some strolling Fryars come often here from Kerry. No Popish school.'[48]

Christopher Pearson, Church of Ireland curate, who made the return for the parish of Cill na Martra on 27 March for the 1766 religious census gave the number of Protestant families in the parish as eight, with 92 'Papist'[49] families. Protestant names included Baldwin, Ellmsley, Powell, Warner and White. One Owen Riordan is also returned as Protestant, so there was at least one convert of native stock. Brown, Bohills [Ó Buachalla / Buckley], MacCarthy / Carthy, Connell, Connor, Flyng [Ó Floinn / Flynn], Gould, Hallissey, Healy, Herlihy, Kelleher, Leary, Liehane [Lehane], Luosy [Lucey], Murphy and Riordan are among the 'Papists', all (except Flynn) family names still found in the parish.

We know from Bishop McKenna's Visitation Book that in 1785 the parish was united to Ballyvourney with a chapel in each place. The Ordnance Survey map of 1842 marked 'RC chapel in ruins' in the centre of the village of Cill na Martra, where the Masons' Apron Bar now stands. A chalice still extant in the parish bears the inscription 'Tuathanadroman 1836' so we can infer the existence of a church then.

It appears that as the enforcement of the Penal Laws relaxed the celebration of the Mass moved from the Mass Rock to the Mass-house. The first Mass-house was about two miles from the site of St Lachtain's Cill in Clohina. Later the Mass-house moved to Cill na Martra village. Bishop M. Collins visited in 1828 and wrote: 'I saw the chapel of Tuathnadromin. It is thatched, long and narrow with very low walls. The altar is miserable and altogether unfit ... It is in the form of a cross, and part of it seems to have been lately built. It is altogether clean and comfortable for such a place having been lately whitewashed.' He visted again in 1830 and noted: 'The chapel at Tuathnadromin where the visitation was held thatched and low, altar poor, require a new one, which it will it is hoped be undertaken when that of Ballyvourney is finished.'[50]

Construction of the present church was begun in 1831 and was completed in 1839, with a tower being added in 1895. A bell by J.J. Murphy of Dublin, had earlier been installed in 1873. The steeple was removed in 1952, and subsequently replaced in 1982. The foundation stone was laid by Herbert Baldwin MP, in 1831. His tomb and that of his son is adjacent to the chapel. The original tabernacle was made of wood. It was replaced by a marble one in c.1890. The original is still extant in the safekeeping of the O'Connor family Derrintogher, whose family home had also provided a residence for the priest in 1831. The chapel originally had no seats, no gallery and a wooden altar. The walls, both inside and out, were of rough stone. Fr. William O'Donovan, who erected the tower, also erected the gallery and two confessionals. Seats were made and sold to families for £1 each. He was also responsible for the marble altar and other refurbishments. He had the church plastered by Galways of Macroom, except for the exterior of the north wall which still remains the original rough stone even after the exterior of the church was first painted in 2007.

The next recorded parish priest following Fr. O'Riordan was Fr. Philip Stafford (1803 – 1819). He was followed by Fr. Jeremiah McGrath (1819 – 36) and then an unbroken successions down to today. The first recorded curate is Fr. Tim Twomey (1899 – 1890), although it is known a Fr. Rea was curate in 1875. Fr. Rea was followed by Fr. David Barry who died in Cill na Martra and was buried in his native Glanworth. Fr. Twomey became PP when Fr. Godwin Lane was declining in health due to age.

The residence of Fr. Riordan is unknown. Fr. Stafford lived with the Gould family in Dromonig and for a time at Cronin's, Caherdaha. Frs. McGrath, Michael Lane (1836 – 45) and Burton

(1845 – 1858) lived at what is now Coughlans, Ballyvoige. Fr. Burton sold this property to his nephew, Lee. Up until the early decades of the 20th century it was still known as 'Matt Lee's'

Fr. Michael Lane was one of the last of the Penal era priests, 'He was one of the few surviving priests in the south who had said Mass in the open air with the people kneeling on the cold damp ground'.[51] The *Cork Examiner* of 3 February 1875 carried a full obituary on his death.

His nephew, Fr. Godwin Lane (1867 – 1889) is buried under the floor of the church. He lived in Carrigaphooka, just outside the parish, in a house he got from the local landlord, Minhear. This house had been built as a clerical residence in 1845. A Fr. Greene lived there before him; this priest never served in Cill na Martra. In summertime, Fr Lane used to cross the Sullane on horseback on his way to Cill na Martra to say Mass. At other times he came by buggy. The road up to Cill na Martra village is still known locally as Nóra Mhór's from a woman who lived at the side of this hill. Fr Lane used to give the lady a lift to Sunday mass. Each time he stopped for her, she would say: 'you are an awful bother to me, Father'; meaning of course that she was a bother to him, but her grasp of English let her down.

This is an interesting anecdote as it shows that many of the people at that time had only broken English, if at all. It also shows that authority figures such as the clergy were functioning totally in English. Fr. Godwin Lane had a reputation of being a saintly man and had a somewhat chequered career. A native of Berrings, he had been a curate in Aghina. While there, his popularity almost caused a schism locally as the people wanted him to be made parish priest when the incumbent died. Leader, the local landlord who was a Protesant, even built a church for him on his estate. Following his burial under the floor of Cill na Martra church, a legend grew up in the Donoughmore area of a ghost funeral from Cill na Martra to Donoughmore so his body would lie beside that of his uncle, Fr. Michael, who was buried there.

During church renovations in 1921, the backdrop to the altar was discovered to be a large picture disguised by a black dye. At lunch-time on 12 March of that year the painter, Patrick J. Daly of Cork, decided he would see if anything lay behing the black facade. He cleaned it and discovered a copy of a Rubens. He signed his name and the date on the picture frame, along with local youth Peter Murphy, son of the sacristan, who was also present.

The original Rubens hangs as part of a triptych 'The Raising of the Cross' in Antwerp Cathedral. Rubens painted this original in 1609 –10. It was seized by the French but returned to Antwerp in 1815. Before Rubens' work, the raising of the Cross had hardly ever been the subject of a painting or sculpture. Art historians view this work as defining Catholic self-confidence during the Counter-Reformation. It is known that Fr. Stafford was in France at the time of the Revolution. Legend has it that he was for a short time chaplain to Marie Antionette and was given the picture by a member of the royal family. He is said to have camouflaged the picture when fleeing to Ireland. Fr. Stafford is buried in the Gould family plot in Dundarierke graveyard, where the gravestone records his death on 17 March 1820, aged 72. His skull was on top of one of the confession boxes in the church up to recent years. Following renovations it was first housed behind a glass panel at the bottom of the gallery stairs and later covered from public view.

His successor, Fr. McGrath, is said to have evicted three tenants and 'grabbed' 70 acres of land. The story recalls that an old woman cursed him at the eviction with Spotted Fever. The bishop, on hearing of the events, moved him to Macroom where he fell ill. The tale goes that local doctors could not diagnose his illness but an army doctor with foreign service from the British garrison diagnosed Spotted Fever. Fr. McGrath is reputed to have been incarcerated in Macroom Workhouse for fear of contagion. He is said to have died there.

When Bishop Keane visited Cill na Martra in 1859 he noted: 'One good chapel and a second wanted'. The second one was built at Renaniree during the years 1866 – 1869. The then parish priest, Fr. Thomas Ahern, wanted to build the second church at Clohina on the site of the Cill Lachtain but the people at the western end of the parish preferred Renaniree as a more convenient location. The parish priest then apparently washed his hands of the whole affair and left the construction to the people. The result was that the edifice was too small and it had to be extended again in 1902.

The church was built by local voluntary labour and was finally completed in 1869. When the roofless structure was completed, the newly-opened Cork-Macroom railway offered to bring timber and slate from Cork for free. However a meeting of local farmers decided the train would not be big enough so a convoy of 50 carts pulled by horses set off for Cork to collect the materials. Renaniree is reputed to be the highest church in the diocese of Cloyne at 685 feet above sea level. In the early years it was known as Séipéal na hAdhairce as, in the absence of a bell, a horn was used to summon the faithful.

An indication of social conditions just after the Famine is that the first horse-cart came to Renaniree in 1848. The family from Gortanimill who ordered it had to carry it home on their backs and got the wheels sometime later.

Notes and references

[1] Lucius J. Emerson, *The March of O'Sullivan Beare*, n.d., p.20

[2] Aodh de Blácam, *Cúltroid Uí Shúilleabháin Bhéara: The Great Retreat*, 1987, p.46

[3] Robert C. Simington, *The Civil Survey AD 1654-1656*, 1942, p.vii

[4] My thanks to Dr. Colin Rynne of the Archaeology Dept. UCC for confirming this in a conversation with me

[5] Toby Barnard, *A Guide to Sources For the History of Material Culture in Ireland 1500-2000*, 2005, p.40

[6] David Dickson, *Old World Colony: Cork and South Munster 1630-1830*, 2005, p.227

[7] TCD MSS Collection: MS 823, fol., 222 and MS 825, fols., 109 and 127

[8] Simington, *op. cit.*, p.355

[9] *ibid.*

[10] *ibid.*

[11] See Joseph Byrne, *Byrne's Dictionary of Irish Local History: from earliest times to c. 1900*, 2004, p.87

[12] Butler, *op. cit.*, p.282

[13] Simington, *op. cit.*, p.357

[14] *ibid.*, p.338

[15] *ibid.*, p.347

[16] Butler, *op. cit.*, p.280

[17] Simington, *op. cit.*, p.337

[18] Butler, *op. cit.*, p.282

[19] *ibid.*, p.254

[20] *ibid.*, p.256

[21] TCD MSS n.1.3. *Analecta Hibernica*, No. 22, 1960

[22] Samuel Hayman, 'Notes on the family of Greatrakes', 1863

[23] *The Intelligencer* 27 July 1665

[24] James Buckley, 'Selections from a General Account Book of Valentine Greatrakes, A.D. 1663-1679', 1908, p.211

[25] sic. This presumably should read 66 & 67

[26] Daniel Beaumont, 'Greatrakes "the stroaker"', *History Ireland*, January/February, 2007, p.66. *Blackwater Angel* was written by John Nolan

[27] C.J.F. McCarthy, 'Baldwins Hold Lot of Kilnamartyra', *Southern Star* 1 August 1970

[28] *Cill na Martra*, 1995, pp.80-83

[29] See Sinead McCoole, 'The Herberts of Muckross', 2005

[30] Tim Cadogan and Jeremiah Falvey, *A Biographical Dictionary of Cork*, 2006, p.11

[31] Pádraig Ó Maidín, 'A lively Cork meeting of 1837', *Cork Examiner* 3 May 1972

[32] Seán Ó Tuama, *Caoineadh Airt Uí Laoghaire*, 1979, p.73

[33] *ibid.*, p.80

[34] *ibid.*, p.16

[35] See Pádraig Ó Maidín quoting Richard Caulfield in 'Death of Art Ó Laoghaire', *Cork Examiner* 4 May 1970

[36] Pádraig Ó Maidín, 'A Parish Priest of Macroom', *Cork Examiner* 16 October 1968

[37] See Peter O'Leary, 'The Life and Times of Art Ó Laoghaire', *Ballingeary History Society*, 1998

[38] Ó Tuama, *op. cit.*, p.8

[39] Rachel Bromwich, 'The Keen for Art O'Leary, Its Background and Its Place in the Tradition of Gaelic Keening', 1947/48, pp.239-40

[40] *ibid.*, p.244

[41] *ibid.*, p.247

[42] *ibid.*, p.249

[43] www.leevalleyireland.com/journal1998/TheLifeAndTimesOfArtOLeary.htm

[44] Breandán Ó Buachalla, 'The Making of a Cork Jacobite', 1993, p.485

[45] *ibid.*, p.472

[46] *ibid.*, p.479

[47] James Buckley, 'The Parish Priests of Counties Cork and Kerry in 1740' [sic], 1900. Note: the title of this article as published contains a typographical error as 1704 is clearly the year in question, not 1740

[48] *Cill na Martra*, 1995, pp.2-3

[49] The originals of this Census were destroyed in the Four Courts in 1922. Some extracts survive; these can be found on www.corkancestors.com

[50] *Diocese of Cloyne AD 2002*, pp.70-1

[51] Rev. James Coombes, 'Catholic Churches of the Nineteenth Century: Some Newspaper Sources', 1975, p.2

CHAPTER 6: THE 19TH CENTURY: INCOMPLETE CONQUEST, LAND & FAMINE

A hundred years after the new Ascendancy rose to power in 1690 relations between planter and native were still disrupted. With ongoing tensions in relation to land and religion the settler class were always aware of the need to arm themselves against the natives.

In the Munster Volunteer Registry of 1782 there is an account of the different Volunteer Corps. The landlords of Muskerry formed the Muskerry Blue Light Dragoons on 1 June 1778. Commanded by Col. Robert Warren, it had a uniform of white jackets edged with blue, and blue lapels edged in white with silver epaulets. The other senior officers were Robert Hutchinson as Lieutenant-Colonel and Samuel Swete as Major. It consisted of one Troop only, which held monthly parades at Carrigadrohid.

Numbers had expanded by 1796 when the Orderly Book of the First Troop of the Muskerry Legion of Yeomanry Cavalry recorded among its ranks Walter Baldwin of 'Clohinco' [Clohina] and Robert Ashe of Ashgrove as privates in the ranks.

Following on from the arrival of Wolfe Tone at Bantry in 1796, the unrest continued with the killing of Robert Hutchinson in 1799 during a raid on his house at Codrum. The story of how Malachy Duggan informed on his comrades is still well-known. Cormac MacCarthy, who had shot Hutchinson on Duggan's orders was one of those he betrayed. He also falsely implicated Cormac's two brothers – Ceallachán and Tadhg – so as to protect himself from any retribution from them. Malachy's cousin John Duggan and the three MacCarthy brothers were among those hanged for the killing in the square in Macroom. The *Hibernian Chronicle* of 13 May 1799 linked the men with 'the exterminating system of United Irishmen', but it is unlikely they were members of that organisation. They were part of the Rockite or Whiteboy movement linked with agrarian unrest. The hangings began in May of 1799 and continued until April of 1802 when David Breen was the last to be hanged.

The three MacCarthy brothers were beheaded after the executions and their heads placed on spikes over the Bridewell in Macroom. They were still there when An t-Athair Peadar Ó Laoghaire was a boy. In his autobiography *Mo Scéal Féin*, he recounts standing at the bridge in Macroom:

> 'Bhí mé ag féachaint anonn ar an gcaisleán…
> Chonaic mé ar aghaidh an chaisleáin amach …
> teach éigin mór agus ballaí árda daingeana ina
> thimpeall, agus trí shlat chaola árda ina seasamh
> in airde as, agus mar a bheadh liathróidín dubh
> in airde ar fad ar bharr gach slaite acu. B'shin
> iad trí cinn na bhfear a crochadh mar gheall ar
> Mh'leachlainn Ó Dúgáin. Cárthaigh ab ea iad
> …'[1]

The bodies of the three MacCarthys are buried in Dundarierke graveyard.[2] In 2000 a monument to those executed was unveiled at Macroom castle.

Following on from the Hutchinson affair, the settlers were sufficiently alarmed that by 1803 one half of the Muskerry Legion was on permanent duty, with garrisons being maintained in Inchigeela and Macroom. In April 1804 the British government, finding itself short of manpower, asked the Muskerry Volunteers to volunteer for foreign service. They politely declined the opportunity – their military ardour was solely to maintain their own position. Samuel Swete wrote in response to the request that 'their not volunteering to go out of their district at present does not arise from any hesitation or tardiness on their part to come forward to meet the enemies of their King and country ... but solely springs from their anxiety to watch over and guard their families and properties which are tolerably extensive, and to the protection of which they humbly conceive ten times the number of any other species of his Majesty's forces may not be equally competent.'[3]

The Nineteenth Century: Tithes, Famine and Land

The Composition Act of 1823 laid down that tithes due to the Established Church which had previously been paid – or extracted – in kind, should henceforth be paid in cash. This was a response to the growing inability of Protestant clergy to extract tithes from a populace which greatly resented and resisted such an imposition. Now it would be the forces of the State which extracted the tithe.

It was decided by the authorities to undertake a valuation of each civil parish in the country to determine how much each landowner would be levied. To add to the iniquity of a tax to support an alien church, the tithe was not levied equally on all lands or even on a sliding scale according to the productivity of the land. Instead some types of land were exempted so that the tithe fell disproportionately on the lower classes.

Resentment of the tithe was universal and this led to an organised and widespread campaign of resistance, resulting in the so-called Tithe Wars. Refusal to pay was so widespread that a compensation scheme for Church of Ireland clergy was introduced to cover their loss of income. Called the 'Clergy Relief Fund 1831' it was set up by an 1832 Act of Parliament. To avail of this, an applicant had to produce a list of tithe defaulters to show

how much he was owed.

Thus we read in an affidavit for the civil parish of Clondrohid of 'immense assemblages of people' in numerous places such as 'Millstreet, Macroom, Kanturk, Kilmichael, Ballyvourney, Ahabullogue, Enniskeen, Kilnamiurtery [Kilnamartrya] etc.' where 'all assembled in an unlawful, riotous & threatening manner declaring they would pay no more tithes & forbidding any person to pay tithes, to act as Auctioneers or to be bidders for any cattle seized...'

Among the long list of names appended as defaulters are:
Daniel Connell, English Garden
Daniel Creedon, Caundromy [Candroma]
Andrew, James and Patrick Golden, Dromagarra [Dromagaree]
Edmund Gould, Prohus
Ellen Healy, widow, Prohus
John, Timothy and Cornelius Riordan, Dromagarra
Cornelius and Timothy Lyhane, Caundromy
James and Tim M'Carthy, Caundromy
Owen M'Carthy, Prohus
John Shorten, Prohus
Mat and Tim Twomey, Ashgrove
William Welply, Prohus.

It is noticeable that Richard Ashe Esq, of Ashgrove, local landlord and also a Protestant, is also listed. It would appear that Protestants also took advantage of the Tithe War to evade paying the tithe, even though they were members of the church whose clergy the tithe was to support. This tactic appears to have been common throughout the country. For example John Butler, Marquess of Ormonde (and one of the richest men in the country) is listed as a tithe defaulter in the parishes of Dunmore and Inistioge, Co Kilkenny, in 1831.

A document signed on 6 July 1826 by Edward Ashe and John Warren, as Commissioners for the tithes of 'Kilnamartery' parish certifies 'the true and just assessment' for all within the parish. The Applotment of the Amount of Composition of the Tithe which was payable to Rev. John Charles Mongan 'Incumbent of said Parish' outlines the amount due from each landholder. The overall valuation of the parish was £4,200, giving £420 as the tithe payable from the parish.

Interestingly, one of the largest landowners in the parish was Fr. McGrath, PP, who held just over 84 acres in Ballyvoige and owed a tithe of £58, a considerable sum at that time. This gives credence to tradition of him being a 'grabber'. Another substantial landowner in Ballyvoige, was Henry Neil, with 88 acres, tithed at £55.

Other landholders in the parish included:

		Acres	£	s	d
James & Batt Connell	Lisbeemore	98	19	10	-
Widow Lucey	Lisbeemore	67	8	10	-
Batt Murphy	Ballyvoige	70	27	-	-
Widow Connell	Caherdaha	6	5	2	-
Henry Ashe Esq	Caherdaha	35	28	-	-
Timothy Carty	Derrintogher	90	30	-	-
Charles McCarthy	Ballyvoige	0-2 roods	0	10	-
Richard Browne	Kealfinchen	108	80	-	-
Allen Browne Snr.	Dromreague	44	32	-	-
Allen Browne Jnr	Dromreague	40	32	-	-
Doctor Baldwin	Clohina	52	45	-	-
Abigail Riordain	Clohina	1	0	10	-
John Crowley	Aghacunna	56	13	-	-
Andrew Golden	Caherkereen	62	34	-	-
Timothy Riordan	Brahane	66	48	-	-
John Barry	Dundareirk	50	25	-	-

		Acres	£	s	d
Corns. Murphy	Lackmore	68	25	-	-
Widow Casey	Gortanimel	102	22	-	-
Denis Lucey	Lisbeebeg	80	13	-	-
Daniel Harrington	Knocksaharn	66	38	-	-

The tithe was adjusted from time to time, according to the average price of wheat for the preceding seven years. In a Quarter Sessions held in Bandon on 24 October 1854, the Cill na Martra tithe was reduced to £322 7s. 2 1/8 d.

Thus Cill na Martra featured in the Whiteboy unrest of the time, which came to a climax in Muskerry in 1822. On the 24 January a party of Whiteboys held up the Tralee mail coach 'near the turnpike of Tuath na Droman, five miles to the west of Macroom'[4] and smashed it to pieces. They also severely wounded the coachman and guard with pikes and killed three of the horses. Ó Maidín quotes a letter written from Macroom by one of the landed gentry on that same day. As the letter writer rode by horse to Macroom that morning, he saw people collecting in groups on the hill-tops. He found the town in a state of alarm when he arrived there at about 11.15 a.m. and 'was informed that an account had arrived at about ten o'clock anouncing that the Whiteboys, in large numbers, were collecting in the neighbourhood of Tuath na Droman'.[5]

Robert Hedges Eyre of Macroom castle left the town with a large military force about 3.30 p.m. or 4.00; this force included the Muskerry Cavalry and the Mounted Rifle Brigade which was garrisoned in Macroom. This force surprised the Whiteboys and took over 20 prisoners, nine of whom were later hanged. A number were killed when the military force divided in two and caught the Whiteboys, who were without firearms apart from a single gun, in a cross-fire.

The condition of the common people at that time is shown by

the description of the first casualties which were brought back to Macroom. The bodies were described as being semi-naked, without a shoe or stocking and with scarcely a coat on their backs.

The most famous engagement of that time was at Keimaneigh, immortalised by Máire Bhuí Ní Laoghaire (one of whose daughters, Neil, married Conchubar Ó hAiligheasa of Tuath na Dromann) in *Cath Chéim an Fhia*. This incident had Cill na Martra connections. A party of military and yeoman including, as the poem relates:

> '*Barrett agus Beecher*
> *Hedges agus Sweete*
> *'s na mílte eile leo*'

led by Hedges Eyre of Macroom and White of Bantry were ambushed by a large party of Whiteboys whom they were chasing. The Whiteboys had been scouring the countryside for arms and were camping openly in the mountains. Houses from Macroom to Bandon and on to Bantry had been raided.

Having attacked Ascendency houses in the Bantry district, they withdrew towards Keimeneigh. According to the *Freeman's Journal* of 25 January 1822, there were 800 in the band. The Earl of Bantry (White) let a force to Ballingeary where they came upon the raiders. Such was the strength of the Whiteboys gathered there that the military were forced to retreat back towards Bantry. The *Freeman's Journal* reported they had a narrow escape. The Whiteboys held the high ground and rained boulders down on them. Brian Brennan writes: 'some time during the early stages of the confrontation, two Rockites, Amhlaoibh Lynch from neary Derry [*recte* Derragh], in the parish of Toohandroman and Barry O'Leary from Garryantornora [*recte* Gaortha an Tornóra] were killed.'[6]

This Amhlaoibh Ó Loingsigh was one of three men working

in Reilig Ghobnatan in Ballyvourney when '*an liú a leath i bhfad i gcéin*' was heard and he rushed off to join the battle. After the battle his body was returned to Reilig Ghobnatan for burial. The Whiteboys were usually termed Rockites by themselves. Their leader was from Kilmurry and went by the name Captain Rock. He got Dómhnall Ó Laoghaire who lived east of Keimaneigh to act as lookout. At the first sign of approaching military the lookout was to get upon the nearest rock and let out a '*liú*' or warning shout. The next Whiteboy who heard this was to do likewise and so on until the whole district was warned.

Seamus Walsh from Túirín Dubh and Conchubhar Buí Ó Laoghaire (brother of Máire Bhuí) killed a soldier of the 39th Regiment named John Smith.

The Whiteboys remained camped in the area for several weeks before eventually drifting away home. The authorities rounded up a large number of locals and 36 were sentenced to death. Two of Máire Bhuí's sons were charged with Smith's murder but were released after nine months in Cork County Gaol due to Daniel O'Connell's defence. It can be surmised that the Cill na Martra connection is also to be seen here; as we have seen, O'Connell's aunt Eibhlín Dhubh had a connection to the Uí Laoghaire through her marriage to Art.

The Schools' Folklore Commission 1938 has also recorded another incident from those days. On 28 March 1938 Conchubhar Ó Éalaighthe related how bailiffs came to Caol Fuinseann and seized cattle. All the neighbours gathered 'agus do bhriseadar isteach i bpáirc ar a ghlaodhtar "Páirc an Gholáin"'. It is noteworthy that Páirc an Ghaláin is at the top of of a hill known as Cnocán a' Bhóna, the hill of the cattle-pound. This pound is marked on the Ordnance Survey Map of 1842. The land-agent who was leading the bailiffs was armed. He fired a shot at the owner of the cattle and knocked his hat off. The people thought he had been shot in the head. A man named Seán Ó Conaill rushed at the agent and killed him with a pike. The bailiffs fled, abandoning the cattle. The corpse was put into a barn for the night. A few days later, 'do tháinig na píléirí agus do thógadar mórán daoíne agus do chuireadar isteach san bpriosún iad. Níor thógadar an duine ceart in aon chor.' Eventually Donnachdha Ó Crimín, his brother Conchubhar and Séamas Ó Goillídhe were tried and sent to prison for two years each.

The Famine

In pre-Famine times Cill na Martra was a vibrant, heavily populated area as the parish records show. In 1803 there were 73 baptisms and 21 marriages. In 1807 there were 108 and nine respectively. In 1811 the figures were 117 and 17. The number of baptisms in the pre-Famine era recorded a high of 140 in 1814, while the highest recorded number of marriages was 36 in 1843. The figures for the Famine years were:

	Baptisms	Marriages
1844	125	17
1845	86	31
1846	-	25
1847	67	4
1848	62	10

No figure for baptisms is recorded for 1846. This seems extraordinary as marriages were still being contracted and recorded. Could it be Famine-related infant mortality swept away all new-borns in that year? The dramatic collapse in the number of marriages from 1844 to 1847 is stark. From 1848 on, the number of marriages falls, often to single digits annually; being as low as three in 1854 and reaching as high as 13 only in

1852 and 1855. It would be 1861 before the recorded figure went as high as 27, a level that would not be attained again for the rest of the 19th century. Indeed the figures fell sharply again for the last two decades of the century, going as low as five in 1887, 1888, 1891 and 1893. These figures tell of mass emigration of young people in the post-Famine years and shows that the effects of the Famine were being felt long after 1848.

The figure for baptisms recorded in 1844 would not be matched again. It had plummetted to 38 in 1851 and would remain in double digits apart from two spikes in 1860 (100) and 1864 (104). Again, the trend of post-Famine decline remains constant, with the number going as low as 30 in 1908, the first decade of the new century.

It is not surprising then that the 1841 census returned a population of 2,782 in 449 households for the parish while the 1851 census shows it dropped to 1,805 persons in 325 households. The Famine set in process a pattern of population decline which continued into the late 20th century and was finally arrested only by the coming of the Celtic Tiger of modern times

In 19th century Ireland famines, both localised and more widespread, were a recurring phenomenon. In the 120 years up to 1848 there were over 20 widespread failures of the potato crop, the staple food of the ordinary people. This reliance on the potato, was summed up in the popular ditty:

> 'prátaí ar maidin 's prátaí um nóin
> 's dá n-eireóinn san oíche, prátaí do gheobhainn'.

This is confirmed by the evidence of Fr. Michael Lane, Parish Priest of Cill na Martra and Ballyvourney, to the Devon Commission in 1844 where he stated potatoes alone, taken in two meals per day, were the staple diet of the ordinary people. Fr.

Lane's evidence to the Commission had also outlined the power land-agents held over tenant farmers. He specifically named James Carnegie, agent of Massey H. Massey, as being oppressive. The *Cork Examiner* of 18 August 1844 carried the evidence of an associate of Carnegie's named Philip Rubie. Rubie handed over a paper signed by 30 tenants (of whom at least 10 were illiterate and signed with an X) purporting to deny that Carnegie was 'extorting fees in money, spirits and sugar ...And we futher declare in the strongest manner, that so far from having any charge against Mr Carnegie, that we are more obliged to him than to any man.' The flowery language used shows it was not composed by those whose names were appended to it. Rubie implicitly admitted this when stating 'I explained it in Irish to those who did not understand English'. It seems clear the tenants were pressurised into signing a pre-written statement.

To cater for the prevailing social conditions, the British government enacted the Poor Law (Ireland) Act in 1838, which introduced the English Poor Law model to Ireland. Parishes throughout the country were grouped into Poor Law Unions. 'Unions were compactly designed with a market town at their centre (where the workhouse would usually be situated) and within a suggested radius of ten miles.' [7] Cill na Martra formed part of the Macroom Union which was formally established on 20 December 1839. It was governed by a Board of 25 elected and eight ex-officio Guardians. A Workhouse was erected on a six acre site in Macroom in 1841-42 at a cost of £8,359 for construction plus a further £1,010 for fittings. It was built to a standard design by George Wilkinson, the English Poor Law Commissioners' architect. It was designed to accommodate 600 inmates and was declared fit for the reception of paupers on 1 October 1842. Its first actual admissions were on 13 May 1843 and by the following December it had 138 inmates. It was therefore in position just on the cusp of the Great Famine but would find itself overwhelmed by that catastrophe; at the height of which a store was hired as an auxilary workhouse to hold another 60 inmates.

An t-Athair Peadar Ó Laoghaire of Lios Caragáin in Clondrohid parish has written vividly in *Mo Scéal Féin* of local folk memories of Macroom workhouse:

'An túisce a bhí siad istigh ann scaradh iad go léir ó chéile. Cuireadh an t-athair i measc na bhfear. Cuireadh an mháthair i measc na mban...Bhí an teach go léir, agus a raibh de dhaoine bochta ann, múchta le gach aon saghas breoiteachtaí. Na daoine, chomh tiubh agus a thagaidís isteach nach mór, ag titim le héagruas ...agus iad ag fáil bháis chomh tiubh agus a thagadh an galar orthu.'[8]

As a recent historian of the Famine in Cork has written:

'In Irish folk-memory, the workhouse will forever be inextricably linked with the tragedy of the Great Famine... inmates of... Irish workhouses were frequently subjected to primitive and inhumane conditions, mainly as a consequence of the attitudes and actions of guardians.'[9]

Herbert Baldwin, MD, of Clohina, was the guardian for the Cill na Martra district. As Máire Mac Suibhne points out 'Landlords and other wealthy property owners were invariably nominated to the Boards and, since the cost of running the workhouse was levied on the ratepayers, it was in their best interests to keep expenses to a minimum.'[10]

With the collapse of the potato crop due to blight, public works were initiated. A meeting was held in Maroom on 10 April 1846, to organise public works for the Union district. Fr. Philip Burton who became parish priest of the then joint parish of Cill na Martra and Ballyvourney in 1845, was spokesman for the people. A further meeting was held on 28 August. Fr. Burton informed this meeting that the situation in his parish was so dire that the people could not long hold out unless relief was given. He said the people were 'famishing' and called on the landlords present not to extract rents but to allow the farmers keep their corn for themselves and their labourers. Only James Welply, among whose holdings were Knockroe, Clonclud and Cahirkereen of Cill na Martra parish, was amenable to this. A letter in the *Cork Examiner* of 7 September 1846 signed by 'Humanity' of Dungarvan spoke of the 'most Christian conduct of Mr James Welply of Macroom, for his very considerate and humane treatment of his conacre and other tenants, forgiving the former their rent and cost of manure, and desiring the latter to keep their corn for the ensuing season's food for their families.'

This attitude of Welply's may be explained by the fact that, despite the surname the family was actually of native MacCarthy stock - the old proprietors of the district. John O'Hart in volume I of his *Pedigrees* tells that Cormac McCarthy (died c.1761), son of Finghin McCarthy Mór, married Dela, daughter and heiress of Joseph Welply (*alias* Guelph) originally from Wales, who - ironically - got some of the confiscated MacCarthy lands in Muskerry. 'Cormac succeeded to Welply's possessions, assumed the name of his father-in-law and was generally called "Welply MacCarthy".'[11] In a footnote, O'Hart, also tells us that a later Welply (William) 'lived at Prohurus [Prohus] near Macroom, and was married to a Miss Scrivener, from Kerry'.[12]

In a similar vein, the *Cork Examiner* of 15 May 1843 recorded a contribution of £2 from James Welply to O'Connell's 'Repeal Rent'.

With the taking of corn for rent, starvation was inevitable. Another letter to the *Cork Examiner* tells us that on 20 November 1846 about four o'clock 'a number of the most miserable and wretched creatures the eye could look on' marched from Cill na Martra and Ballyvourney to Macroom and went to the bakers' shops looking for food. On 20 February 1847 Fr. William McCarthy, curate to Fr. Burton, wrote to the *Cork Examiner* telling how a 'poor man, by name Herlihy, died of actual starvation at Culavokig.'

On Friday 5 March 1847 the *Cork Examiner* carried the account of a reporter who toured the parish the previous Sunday with Fr. Burton 'the better to acquaint myself with the destruction of Kilnamartery'. In Derrintogher they went to the cabin of Daniel Quinlan, a labourer with a wife and nine children. 'Nothing could equal the destitution and desolation that prevailed in this hut of want and woe …Every member of the family, with the exception of one grown-up lad, was "down in the sickness".' Then they went to the hovel of Darby Leary. 'Leary, stretched by the chimney-corner was fast hastening to dissolution, his eyes being fixed with glassy, whilst, to judge from appearances, his wretched wife could not long survive him.'

Fr. Burton told the reporter how he had found a girl of 12 or 13 dead in the house of Owen Swiney of Ballyvoige, while the parents were so weak from hunger and sickness they could not arise to go to the child. A few days later, another daughter aged 10 or 11 also died.

In the home of Daniel Lehane they found 'pining and slowly decaying no less a number than fifteen human beings' comprising the Lehane family and their neighbours, who had left their own hovel at Fr. Burton's urging only the day before it collapsed. Lehane has failed to get employment on the public works; the family had also failed to gain entry to the workhouse and had returned home to die. At the time of the reporter's visit, they hadn't eaten in 48 hours; all they had by way of sustenance was warm water with a handful of salt in it.

The reporter stated he had not described one-fourth of the

cases he had witnessed. He also gave a listing of other deaths in the parish: Patrick Murray dropped on the road while returning from the Public Works and died within minutes; Daniel Lucey was found speechless on the roadside by Mr. Ashe of Dromonig, having lain there all night; he died a few hours later. Thomas Murray, Patrick Hallisey and John Conell all died even though employed by the Board of Works as 'their weekly stipend was insufficient to support nature'. Readers were told that the names of many others, adults as well as minors, could be added to his list. 'So much for Kilnamartery', the report bleakly concludes.

The Public Works in the parish was a new road to Ballyvourney, through Cools and Knocksaharn. Local historian Máire Uí Thuama, through whose family farm it ran, recalls that in 'my young days there was a field which we always called "Scionn a' bhóthair" meaning "An pháirc ós cionn an bhóthair" - the field above the road. The road was was distinctly defined with a fence on either side, it was a road that went nowhere.'[13] A line of roadway, some three miles long, also meandered through Derrintogher, Ballyvoige, Kylefinchin and Knockroe.

A soup-kitchen was also set up in the village, where Cooney's house now stands. This was presumbably an initiative of the local Famine relief committee. The *Cork Examiner* of 24 February 1847 records subscriptions to the 'Kilnamartery Parish Famine Relief Fund Committee'. The Rev. Mr. Crofton and Rev. Mr. Brown led the list with contributions of £10 and £5 respectively. Local landlords Edward Ashe and Herbert Baldwin JP gave £3 each. Fr. Burton donated £2 10 s., while his curate Fr. McCarthy gave £1. Local farmers Allen Brown, Tim and Mat Twomey and John Gould also gave £1 each. Thomas Connor and Widow Connell gave 10 s. J.W. Baldwin, Clerk, Treasurer, 'earnestly requested that those landlords who have been written to, and have not yet answered, may do so soon, as it is intended to forward the list to Government for an equivalent sum, as the circumstances of the parish are truly distressing.'

The *Cork Examiner* of 25 May 1846, carried an account of a coursing meeting in Ballyvourney where 'Sir G. Colhurst's red dog, Grasshopper, beat Mr.Welply's black dog, George', showing that life continued on with relative normality for the upper tier in society.

On 24 Februay 1847 an extraordinary Presentment Sessions – the forum where relief works were proposed – was held at Macroom. Land proprietors from the Barony of West Muskerry along with the Catholic and Protestant clergy and numbers of various Relief Committees were in attendance. Fr. Burton and others condemned Captain Gordon, the Board of Works engineer, for his treatment of labourers on relief works. They frequently had to wait three weeks for pay – which might explain some of the deaths noted above for those in such employment. Fr. McCarthy had alluded this in his letter to the *Cork Examiner* where he described the people as 'like moving skeletons as they go to and from the road works …Three weeks' wages are usually due before they see the face of wage clerk.'

It was against this backdrop that on 5 April 1847 Fr. Burton wrote to the *Cork Examiner* stating that 'dysentry and dropsy, the necessary consequence of famine, are making frightful havoc among our emaciated poor people. I have today been called to attend ten sick people where in many instances I found the living and the dead thrown on a common litter of filthy straw'. He concluded that 'Every man who is able is flying to America'. Even that avenue of escape had its dangers: 'Nora Healy, Rahoona, Cill na Martra, died of famine fever on board ship in 1847 or 1848. She was buried at sea.'[14]

The Famine altered the social and physical landscape of the parish. 'Clochars' were a feature of pre-Famine Cill na Martra. These were clusters of cabins, inhabited by the cottier class who held no land themselves. These people were the first to fall prey to starvation and were more or less wiped out as a class. The faint remains of a clochar of about ten cabins is recorded at the top of Árd a' Bhóna. A hamlet of 12 cabins known as An Cuasán also existed in upper Coolavokig. Its demise is traced not to the Famine but to the fact that its centre-point and *raison d'etre*, a forge, accidentally took fire and burnt to the ground. With it went the hamlet's commercial centre and it decayed.

The Famine was also a blow to the landlord class which, absentee or not, relied on rents to finance their lifestyle. When these incomes collapsed during the Famine it had serious financial implications for this class. Their dependence on rental incomes is illustrated by a notice which appeared in the *Cork Examiner* of 18 January 1843 on the eve of the Famine: 'The several Persons liable to the Payment of RENT-CHARGE in the Parishes of KILNAMARTERY, DRISHANE and NOHOVAL DALY, are requested to forward the amount of their NOVEMBER ACCOUNTS and ARREARS to Herbert E. O'Donnell, Solicitor, Macroom, and 21 North Cumberland Street, Dublin, whom I have appointed as my Agent, with full authority to Collect and Receive the same – dated this 16th day of January, 1843 – John Charles Mongan, Clerk, Rector of Kilnamartery, &c, &c'. Thus the Encumbered Estates Acts of 1848 and 1849 were passed to allow for the sale of estates that were effectively bankrupt. Before these Acts, such land sales were inhibited by legal procedures involving lengthy title searches, etc. The Landed Estates Court was set up to process these sales, of which there would be more than 3,000 bewoen 1849 and 1857.

Among these was the sale of the estate of Richard Ashe of Ashgrove and Alicia, his wife. It was sold at auction by the Commissioners for Sale of Incumbered Estates in Ireland at their Court at no. 14 Henrietta St., Dublin, at 12.00 noon on Tuesday 10 December 1850. Included in the specification of lands were East and West Dromony [Dromonig] where Timothy Twomey was a tenant holding 94 acres at a yearly rent of £105 and 12s., payable on Gale days 1 May and 1 November. As part of the lease the tenant was obliged to lay 100 barrels of 'well-burnt running kiln lime' on the land each year. The lease also held a covenant that the tenant could not sub-let any of the land. The landlord also held for himself all mines, minerals and royalties of these lands was well as the hunting, fowling, fishing, coursing and sporting on the lands.

The Encumbered Estates records also show that Leslie Craggs O'Callaghan, owner of dwelling houses in the Mardyke and Hanover Street in Cork as well as property in Carrigrohane also owned lands in Ashgrove at this period.

Griffith's Valuation

The Primary Valuation of Tenements, usually called *Griffith's Valuation* lists occupiers of land and houses. It was carried out between 1848 and 1864 and was a national survey for the purposes of establishing the level of rates to be levied on each property holder or leaseholder. In effect it serves as a census substitute for each area in the period immediately after the Famine, though of course it does not list everybody, only property holders.

Under the Irish Poor Law Act of 1838, a valuation of each tenement was authorised to allow for the assessment of a 'poor rate' to fund the Poor Law Unions. The valuations of the Unions of Dunmanway, Millstreet and Macroom (of which Cill na Martra formed part) was published by Griffith at the General Valuation Office in Dublin on 30 November 1852. It shows some interesting facts about Cill na Martra.

Rev. John Mongan, who, as we have seen, was Church of Ireland incumbent for tithes, and who was to die in Belize, was an absentee who held the church and graveyard (1 rood and 36 perches) at the Glebe with a rateable valuation of £5. The church and graveyard were exempted from actually paying the rate. He also held a house, offices (outhouses) and land (2 acres, 2 roods and 6 perches) with a rateable valuation of £1 10 s. for the land and a huge £12 for the house. These were sublet to the Rev. John M. Whiting. This glebe house is stated to have been derelict by 1860.[15] Mongan also had further lands at the Glebe, just over 37 acres valued at £20 15 s. let to the Rev. Henry Swanzy. Swanzy also held a house (unoccupied) valued at 4 s.; he also had another house and garden (rated at 5 s. each) leased to Susan Harrington. Swanzy also rented a house, offices and land (133 acres) in Raleigh South from Dr. John Leader; also in Raleigh South, Swanzy had two houses leased to William Walsh and John Croneen; he also held one other unoccupied house. Given its being an uncommon surname, could this Rev. Swanzy be a forebear of District Inspector Oswald Swanzy who was involved in the murder of Tomás MacCurtain nearly 70 years later?

In the townland of Lackmore, Cornelius Murphy had a house, offices, and land (just over 66 acres) from Massey H. Massey; the buildings were rated at £1, the land at £19. Con Murphy also had two houses for lease – one unoccupied valued at 4 s.; the other leased to John Leahy and valued at 8s.

In Renanirce, Herbert Baldwin had leased a National School house, office and yard valued at £1 15 s. to Cornelius Cronin, teacher. The school was exempted from actually paying the rate.

Ellen Dineen had over 107 acres along with a house and offices leased from Baldwin, rated at £18. She also had a house valued at 4 s. leased to Patrick Sullivan.

Edward Ashe had a house, offices and over 190 acres leased from Rev. Robert Gray in Candroma, the whole valued at £65 10 s. Ashe had property leased to Jeremiah Lehane, Timothy Cronin, Catherine Cronin, Timothy Lehane and Cornelius Lehane.

Henry Brown had a house, offices, and over 160 acres (valued at £83 15 s.) from Stephen Graham in Raleigh South. In turn he had no less than seven houses – three with gardens – leased out to others. John Leader MD had over 45 acres along with a house and offices (the total valued at £ 23 15 s.) leased to John Brae in the same townland.

In Lisboy More, Rev. John Brown had four separate plots of land, one with house and offices, leased jointly to Daniel and James Connell. Rev. Brown also had other property leased to Timothy Delaney, Margaret Connell, and Jeremiah Sweeney. He also had property leased to combinations of people. One plot of land of just over six acres and valued at £1 was jointly leased to Daniel Leehane, Patrick Ring, Denis Buckley, John Buckley and Patrick Buckley. This is a type of landholding not often adverted to in the literature.

This same combination had a separtate lease on a house, offices and land totalling just over 46 acres, also from Rev. Brown. Brown also leased other property in Lisboy More to other combinations with from two to seven members.

In Raleigh North, James Minhear rented separate properties to John Murphy, Johanna Purcell, William Delany and John Buckley.

In the Bantry House archive, which was donated to UCC some years ago, the earliest document is a lease dated 30 August 1720 between Sir Richard Cox of Dunmanway and Thomas Howard of Raleigh regarding the lands of 'Coolavohig, Barony of Muskerry'. The Howard name had gone from Raleigh by Griffith's time.

C.J.F. McCarthy, writing in the *Southern Star* of 15 August 1970 refers to an Aghacunna Estate map of 1844 showing part of the Edward Ashe estate. The map shows 18 farms in 1844. By the time of Griffith, Thomas Brown was the lessor of most of this townland. He had properties leased to Jeremiah Casey, Timothy Leary, Julia Leary, Jeremiah Crowley, Ellen Murphy, John

Dennehy, James Quill and John Meany. The change between 1844 and 1852 was no doubt a direct result of the Famine. The names of tenants Horgan and Crowley had remained but Lyhane, Riordan and Delany had gone.

In 1852, James Welply held just over 6 roods of land in Ahacunna, 'in fee', valued at 8 s. He had more substantial holdings in Clonclud where he had over 34 acres leased to Matthew Connor. Other Welply tenants here were Henry Brown (house, offices and land valued at £29) and Francis Lehane who had a house and garden valued at 5 s. He also had property leased to tenants in Knockroe, though Griffith's scribe spells his name 'Whelply' here. In this townland he himself also held 'in fee' a dairyhouse and 50 acres of land, valued at £7. Tenants of Welply in Caherkereen were John Gould, Michael Gould, John Murphy and Daniel Goolding.

In Coolcaum, Welply himself held offices and over 260 acres of land valued at £88. He also had seven unoccupied houses for lease here. C.J.F. McCarthy posits a Famine clearance here. Welply also had other houses (some with gardens) valued from 2 s. to 6 s., leased to Judith Sullivan, John Reddon, William Sweeney and John Murphy. The description of house with garden means cabin with potato plot. As mentioned before, this cottier class was the most affected by the Famine and here in Coolcaum we see the results in microcosm. This is all the more forceful when we recall Welply had done more than other landlords to help his tenants at that time.

Dromreague townland held a total of 14 such house and garden tenements, the area of the whole being as low as eight perches in one case. By contrast, W.G. Brown held over 117 acres here along with a house and offices. William Brown held just over 89 acres.

Derryfineen also had a high concentration of cottiers with 11 such holdings. The on-going plight of these people post-Famine is highlighted in the case of William Duggan of Derrintogher who held a house and garden, the whole amounting to an area of 12 perches, but who found himself facing a rate of 5 s. under Griffith.

In Cloheena [Clohina] Herbert Baldwin M.D. held three separate plots of offices and land (251 acres, 153 acres and 46 acres respectively) totalling £121 5 s. in valuation. He had eight cottier-type plots for lease, four of which were unoccupied. Again we can view this as a legacy of the Famine. One of his more substantial tenants was Denis Kelly who leased over 64 acres along with a house and offices, the whole being rated at £24 5 s.

At the end of the scale, Thomas Murray, John Mangan, Jeremiah Hallissey and Catherine Lucey each rented a house and garden from John Connell in Caherdaha and were faced with valuations from 2 s. to 12 s.

Notes and References

[1] An t-Athair Peadar Ó Laoghaire, *Mo Scéal Féin,* [gan data; eagrán caighdeánaithe], p.50

[2] Dáithí agus Seán MacSuibhne (cnuasaitheoirí), *Slí na Staire i gCill na Martra*, 2006, p.35

[3] Robert Day, 'First Muskerry Cavalry. Notes from the Orderly Book of the First Troop of the Muskerry Legion of Yeomanry Cavalry, 1796, with reduced facsimile of page of Orderly Book', 1896, p.5

[4] P. Ó Maidín, 'A battle near Macroom in 1822', *Cork Examiner* 24 January 1972

[5] *ibid.*

[6] Brian Brennan, *Máire Bhuí Ní Laoire: A Poet of her People*, 2000, p.37

[7] Michelle O'Mahony, *Famine in Cork City*, 2005, p.17

[8] An t-Ath. P. Ó Laoghaire, *op. cit.*, p.37

[9] Colman O'Mahony, *Cork's Poor Law Palace: Workhouse Life 1838-90*, 2005, p.295

[10] Máire MacSuibhne, *Famine in Muskerry: An Drochshaol*, 1997, p.19

[11] John O'Hart, *Irish Pedigrees: or The Origin & Stem of the Irish Nation*, Vol. I, 1915, p.115

[12] *ibid.*, footnote

[13] *Cill na Martra*, p.76

[14] Máire MacSuibhne, *op. cit.*, p.92

[15] *Cill na Martra*, p.43

CHAPTER 7 : GLIMPSES OF CILL NA MARTRA IN THE 19TH AND 20TH CENTURIES

In 1844 *The Parliamentary Gazetter of Ireland*, listed 'Kilnamartry, or Kilnamartery' as a parish being eight miles in length and two in breadth with an area of 11,680 acres. The population in 1831 is given as 2,604, while 10 years later in 1841 it is given as 2,782, with 435 houses in the parish. The tithe composition was £420 plus a glebe of £30, giving the rector a gross income of £450, the net income is given as £357 13 s. 5 ½ d. The rector 'holds also the benefice of Drishane in the dio. [diocese] of Ardfert and Aghadoe, but is resident in Kilnamartry'.

In 1591 40 acres were granted to a Protestant rector on his appointment to Cill na Marta church and 'parish records show an unbroken succession of Rectors until Cill na Martra was amalgamated with Macroom in 1872.'[1] The same source tells that income in 1774 was £100 and the church was in ruins. 'It seems likely this was a chapel attached to nearby Dún-da-Radharc castle. A new church was built in 1808 with a capacity of 100 at a cost of £1000'.[2] In 1814 a rectory was built, at a cost of £1,300. Despite these building expenses, the congregation never exceeded 20. The *Gazetteer* says that the church was built in 1813 by means of a gift of £553 16 s. 11d. from the Board of First Fruits. While 100 could be accommodated, the actual attendance was 15.

Dundareirke would appear to have been an extension of Protestants from Macroom along the main ridge or old Bealach

Feabhradh into Cill na Martra. The Rev. Horatio Townsend, writing in his 1810 work *Statistical Survey of Co. Cork* spoke of how 'beyond the turn of the century [i.e., 1700] Richard Hedges was building up a Protestant settlement at Macroom...'[3] In an ironic mirror image to this, Catholics from Macroom also came along the same route to attend at Mass rocks in Cill na Martra during the Penal era.[4]

The *Gazetteer* notes that the Roman Catholic chapel 'has an attendance of 1,500; and is united to the chapel of Ballyvourney'. It also notes '4 daily schools – one of which was salaried with £3 from subscription and £15 from the National Board – were usually attended by about 243 children'.

We know from the 1826 Report of the Commissioners on Irish Education that there was a pay-school in Lackmore, run by Patrick Murphy. 100 pupils were in attendance, in a building (no longer extant) valued at £10. Parents paid the teacher £4 11 s. The same report also lists a school in Shanballyshane at the other end of the parish. This school had 80 children and parents paid a total of £12 15 s. per annum. This school is stated to be run by Mr. Connell; this was the famous Gaelic scholar and scribe Seán Máistir Ó Conaill who was from Clohina.

There was also a hedge-school in Aghacunna, in the south of the parish, some traces of which still remain. A spot in Knockroe is called Móinteán na Scoile, suggesting the location of a hedge-school but there is no other information extant.

Cill na Martra village also had a school located where the churchyard is now. Building began on this school in 1825. It was a double school-house, one for boys and one for girls. The building cost £50 and therefore must have been of a good standard for the time. It was funded by bequests from the late Fr. Stafford and from Bishop Coppinger. The parish priest Fr. Jeremiah McGrath also contributed monies. Henry Cornwall of Bandon, who was the landlord of the plot where it was located, gave £2. The school was open from 9.00 a.m. to 6.00 p.m., Monday to Saturday but closed in winter. It had an enrollment of 150 pupils and three teachers; pupils 'attended in relays'.[5] Fr. McGrath expressed disappointment that apart from Cornwall who gave £3 per year to give free schooling to children of landless labourers and poorer tenant farmers, the other landlords of the parish gave nothing.

This school was in operation until 1897 when Ballyvoige NS opened under the patronage of Fr. William O'Donovan. Local lore records that a fife and drum band led the pupils through the village from the old school in the churchyard to the new one.

Other National Schools in the parish were located at Dundarierke, Coolavokig and Renaniree. Dundarierke NS was built by Fr. O'Donovan in 1898, using stone from the derelict Church of Ireland in the adjoining graveyard. Fr. O'Donovan (whose nickname 'Bully' gives some insight into his character) had got into a dispute with the neighbouring farmer named Murphy who now blocked his access to the building materials. A standoff ensued until one Sunday at Mass the parish priest announced he had received correspondence from a solicitor in Australia concerning a large amount of money left by a native of the parish called Murphy who had died without an heir. He invited anyone who thought he might be related to contact him in the sacristy after Mass. This particular farmer had an uncle who had emigrated to Australia many years previously so he approached the parish priest. The priest undertook to do all necessary writings to ensure the legacy; he then mentioned the small matter of access. In the bonhomie engendered by the prospect of future riches he was told this would be no problem. The building materials were secured but nothing further was heard about the legacy.

The school in Renaniree was begun in 1841 by Fr. Michael Lane, who had received £50 to build a National School. It opened on 23 September 1842 with 70 pupils.

There had been a school in Coolavokig since the 1820s. The

Commissioners on Irish Education found a school worth £6 taught by Patrick Twomey. It had 32 pupils. A second classroom was added in 1900-1901.

Guy's County and City of Cork Directory 1875-1876 lists John Brown, Cools, among the gentry of the Macroom district, while John W. Browne, also of Cools, was an ale and stout agent. Rev. D. O'Callaghan was Catholic curate in 'Kilnamartery'; while the parish priest, Fr. Godwin Lane resided at Derryfineen. Principal landowners listed included:

Patrick Cronan [sic]   Cahirkereen
Timothy Cronin   Condroma [sic]
Edward Gould   Dromonig
Michael Harrington   Cloonycarthy
Cornelius Kelleher   Clonclud
Edmond Lee   Ballyvoge [sic]
Timothy Lucey   Knocksaharing [sic]
Daniel Murphy   Dundareirke
John Twomey   Dromeague

MR. WM. Duggan,
Kilnamartyra, Macroom, whose death was announced on Monday last, at the age of 112 years

Billy Duggan

There was no post office in Cill na Martra at that time; Ballyvourney, Inchigeela and Kilmichael being the sub-post offices of Macroom. Ballyvoige post office opened in 1883, with Cornelius Riordan as postmaster.

By 1886, *Guy's Postal Directory of Munster* listed 'Ballyvoge' post office, 'parish of Kilnamartery'. The population of the parish is given as 1,861. It describes Cill na Martra as: 'Land generally cold and unproductive, with a large extent of rough rocky pasture, bog and marsh; good building stone and inferior slate raised in several places, and there are indications of copper ore.' Con Riordan was still postmaster. Gentry and clergy of the parish are listed as Fr. Lane, PP, Rev. Laurence Walsh CC and Capt. Thomas L. Leader, Ashgrove.

The head teacher at Ballyvoige NS was Jerh Horgan. Among the principal farmers were:

Patrick Coleman	Candroma
Edmund Goold	Dromonig
Michael Riordan	Dromagarry
Allen Browne	Dromreague
Henry Browne	Cools
Thomas Browne	Clonclud
Daniel Connell	Knocksaharn
Denis Connell	Lisboy
Maurice Connell,	Caherdaha
Patrick Connor	Derrintogher
Timothy Leary,	Aghacunna
Matthew Twomey	Kylefinchin

Guy's Postal Directory County Cork for 1892 noted Robert Warren was now resident gentry at Ashgrove; while shopkeepers M. Connell, vintner, Caherdaha and Daniel Corkery, grocer, are also listed.

The same directory for 1893 notes that a fresh butter mar-

ket was held 'every Saturday at Ballyvogue Cross'. By 1895 two other traders were added: William Johnson, smith, and Margt. Kelleher, vintner.
By 1897 the directory was noting:

>Thomas Browne, grocer
>Denis Buckley, vintner
>Richard Manning, blacksmith
>J. Riordan, vintner.

By 1903 Mrs. C. Riordan, widow of Con Riordan, was listed as postmistress. A legacy of the Land War was the listing of an RIC sergeant at a Constabulary sub-station in Kilmakarogue. The Land League had been active in Cill na Martra, as elsewhere. Galvin records that 8,000 attended a land meeting there on 12 December 1880. An even larger crowd attended a huge meeting in the parish on 4 January 1881 when Parnell was proclaimed the saviour of the people and 'the pillars of oppressive landlordism' were condemned. On the following 9 May the Cill na Martra branch of the Land League held a meeting to condemn the arrest of John Dillon MP and also 'condemned rack renting in the parish as well as town solicitors involved in serving writs...'[6] the Ladies' Land League was also active in the parish, with Mary Twomey being one of its more fiery leaders.

The fresh butter market was now held every Tuesday and Friday. The commercial life of the village had now expanded to include:

>John Browne, leather merchant
>Miss Browne, dispensary caretaker
>Mary Corkery, milliner and dressmaker
>Katie Creedon, dressmaker.

By 1904, Michael Murphy from Coolea had married into the

Riordan family and was now postmaster.

Changing social trends are clear by 1911 when the only notable 'Residents' are the clergy, Timothy O'Donoghue, PP and Rev. E. Irwin CC. The category of 'gentry' had disappeared. Dr. P. Gould is listed as medical officer. Daniel Murphy, carpenter and Cornelius Sullivan, shopkeeper, have come onto the scene. Listed landholders have significantly increased and now include:

>A. Kelleher, Candroma
>Denis McCarthy, Candroma
>Daniel Golden Dromagarry
>Timothy Riordan, Dromagarry
>John Connell, Knocksaharn
>Matthew Connor, Derrintogher
>Patrick Cooney, Kilmakaroge
>Mrs. Fanny Browne, Ballyvoige
>Daniel Dineen, Knockroe
>Jeremiah Horgan, Ballyvoige
>Charles Vaughan, Kylefinchin

In 1920 Annie Hyde is district nurse and D. Sheehan (father of Seán Ó Síocháin, future General Secretary of the GAA) is among the list of shopkeepers. Landholders included:

>Daniel and Daniel M. Kelleher, Candroma
>Edmund Goold, Dromonig, Member of Cork County Council
>Cornelius Healy, Ballyvoige
>Patrick Buckley DC, Lisboymore
>Peter Sullivan, Ballyvoige

Ballyvoige NS head teachers were John Sullivan and Mrs. Minnie Sullivan, with Miss E. M. O'Shea as Assistant. Miss E. Linehan was in charge of Dunareirke NS. By 1928 Mathew Lucey was head of Ballyvoige NS. Other teachers were listed as Nance O'Sullivan, Miss Nora O'Sullivan and Miss K. Kelleher.

In 1933 Nora O'Sullivan had left and Miss S. Ní Chéilleachair is listed as Assistant. Postmaster Michael Murphy is now listed a second time under the heading 'Residents': along with the clergy Rev. Edwark Shinnick PP and Rev. Barry CC he is listed as 'Murphy, M, professor of Irish'.

By 1944, Guy's had adopted a more democratic format and only the postmaster and the creamery manager, C. Murray, and assistant manager, M. Murphy, were listed by title. All other names were given alphabetically, with occupation (usually 'f' for farmer) afterwards. These include:

> Wm Cullinane Aghacunna
> Mrs. J. Gould, NT
> J. Hyde, Gurteeneadin
> H. Kelleher Shanballyshane
> M. Leahy, Dromreague
> Mrs. Ellie Lucey, Lisbee [sic]
> C. Manning , Cahircareen, carpenter,
> Thos. Murphy, vintner
> J. Vaughan, Kylenfinchin

The Twentieth Century
In a sleeve-note for the music CD, *Guth ar Fán*, by Máire Ní Chéileachair, both of whose parents were from the parish, Cill na Martra is described as 'dúiche nár chloígh riamh le Seán Buí'. This has been true in the political as well as the cultural field. One of the US Civil War veterans who returned to Ireland to partake in the Fenian Rising of 1867 was John O'Connor. He was born in Leac in 1844 and his family emigrated to Massachusetts during the Famine. On his return to Ireland he stayed with his

uncle Thomas O'Connor of Derrintogher. He was arrested by the authorities and sent to Kilmainham Gaol. His American citizenship meant that he was deported to the US rather than imprisoned with the Fenians. He returned to Massachusetts and became a policemen, eventually becoming a captain. The name John O'Connor is inscribed on the panel dedicated to 1867 on the National Monument on the Grand Parade in Cork, showing his importance in Cork Fenian history. In May 1967, the centenary of the Fenian Rising, O'Connor's grandson, John O'Sullivan of Andobea, Massachusetts made his first visit to Ireland.

The IRB connection was continued into the early years of the century. Michael Harrington, of Knocksaharn, was sent to Limerick Gaol for 11 months for illegal Fenian drilling.[7] In 1916 his brother Dan 'Farmer' Harrington led 20 Cill na Martra Volunteers to Carriganima, led by their local fife and drum band, along with Volunteers from the neighbouring districts of Macroom, Clondrohid, Ballinagree and Carriganima to await distribution of arms from the *Aud*.[8]

Florence O'Donoughue, historian and leading member of the Volunteer movement in Cork and head of IRA intelligence in Cork during the War of Independence, wrote a private account of his revolutionary career which has only recently been published. While outlining his role organising the Cork No. 1 Brigade (whose area stretched from Youghal in the east to the county bounds on the west, north to Donoughmore and south to Ballinhassig) in 1919, he recounts a visit to Cill na Martra: '... Tom Crofts and I went out on a Saturday night to the Eighth Battalion and stayed with Patrick O'Sullivan's family at Kilnamartyra. Patrick was the Battalion Commandant and his father, the principal teacher at the local National School. They had a special pew in the church, the first below the altar rails on the Gospel side. We went to mass with some of the family on Sunday morning and sat in the pew with them. The PP... came out of the sacristy before

Mass and took a good look at us. Evidently making up his mind that we were engaged in the same foolish and dangerous business as Patrick he devoted his sermon to warning the young men of the parish against being led astray by strangers, cocking a glaring eye at us now and again. 'No one' he said, 'knows who they are; no one knows where they came from, and no one knows where they are going'. He was by no means unique in his attitude to us at the time. Incidentally, it was the first and last time I ever saw a priest come off the altar during Mass to take up the collection himself.'[9]

The Soloheadbeg ambush in Tipperary on 21 January 1919 is usually accepted as the first armed act of the War of Independence. Desmond Ryan's well-known book on Seán Treacy typically states regarding a Dail resolution of April 1919: 'At the time de Valera spoke – with the exception of the Soloheadbeg ambush three months before-…no attack had been made … on the RIC as a body.'[10]

In fact, the first successful armed action of the War of Independence took place in Cill na Martra parish at Béal a'Ghleanna [The Mouth of the Glen] on Sunday 8 July 1918. (The first shots in the War of Independence were fired in April 1918 at Gortatlea Barracks in Kerry when the Ballymacelligot Co. of the Volunteers attempted an arms raid. These first shots were fired by the RIC and two Volunteers were killed. The raid has been described as a fiasco[11]).

An *Aeríocht* had been organised in Coolea but was proclaimed by the authorities. It is an indicator of the spirit of resistance at the time that it went ahead despite RIC and military being drafted in from all quarters. Among the participants of the *feis* that day was a Gael from Scotland named Ian MacKenzie Kennedy who played the pipes. He would later become an active IRA fighter (known as 'Scotty') and was killed in the Civil War single-handedly holding back Free State forces who had landed at

Monkstown by ship to take Cork City. General Emmett Dalton who commanded the landing party paid tribute later to his bravery. Also during the *feis* in Cooolea *Cath Chéim an Fhia* was one of the songs performed. It would turn out to be an appropriate choice.

Among the contingent drafted in to disrupt the seditious assembly were Constables Bennet and Butler of Ballingeary RIC station. Some seven local Volunteers from Coolea and Ballingeary, including two from Cill na Martra – John Lynch of Béal a'Ghleanna and Dan Tady McSweeney – decided to attack them as they returned to barracks that evening. They had a twofold objective: firstly to destroy the borrowed side-cart they were using for transport so that people would be discouraged from providing co-operation to the authorities; and secondly (as with the explosives being guarded at Soloheadbeg) to get armaments for the coming struggle, in this case two Lee-Metford rifles plus ammunition, as the local company was seriously short of arms. At this period they were mainly equipped with farmers' shotguns and home-made cartridges.

Of the seven Volunteers, only three were armed. They had two .38 revolvers and one shotgun. After a short struggle the RIC men were overpowered, one being shot in the neck but not fatally. The arms were secured and the sidecar thrown into the deep glen. This first successful act of resistance in the independence struggle aptly brought together some strands of local and national history. The ambush took place within metres of the route O'Sullivan Beare took in Elizabethan times, while one of the participants was related to the Amhaoibh Ó Loingsigh killed at Keimaneigh almost a century previously.

Donnchadh Mac Neilus came into the neighbouring district while on the run, following his rescue from Cork Gaol in November 1918. Following a lull, local Volunteers including the 8th Battalion of Cill Martra were active from the start of 1920.

Inchigeela RIC barracks was attacked twice as was Ballingeary barracks.

In July 1920, Cill na Martra and Ballyvourney Volunteers undertook their first ambush of a British military patrol at Geata Bán in Coolavokig. The ambush party had only two service rifles between them, the rest being armed with revolvers and shotguns. The main objective of the ambush was to seize rifles and ammunition. Liam Lynch had used this tactic in Fermoy in 1919. The Geata Bán ambush was unsuccessful but shortly afterwards a military cycle patrol was ambushed at the Slippery Rock on the Ballyvourney / Clondrohid road. The officer in charge was killed and four other soldiers wounded; the others then surrendered. All their arms and equipment were captured. Following these events the 8th Battalion had a well-armed flying column of about 30 men by the autumn of 1920.

The fight between Republican and Crown forces in Cork city has also been intensifying over this period. Finding themselves losing the initiative, the British reverted to the tactic used in the killing of Lord Mayor Tomás MacCurtain: assassination of known or presumed Volunteers. As Borgonovo puts it: 'an important element of the Anglo-Irish conflict in Cork concerns disguised Crown forces, known to city Republicans as 'The Murder Gang'[12]. Peter Hart concurs: 'There is considerable evidence that, as Republicans asserted then and ever since, some sort of death squads had emerged within the RIC by late 1920. There may well have been a regular group of men in Cork ... who carried out extrajudical killings.'[13] These, along with a Loyalist group known as the Anti-Sinn Féin society forced some of the leading city IRA men to move to the western sector of the Brigade area – the Ballingeary / Ballyvourney / Cill na Martra region – where they joined the local column to form a Brigade Flying Column. They included Brigade O/C Seán O'Hegarty, brothers Jim and Miah Grey, Dan 'Sandow ' Donovan and Brigade

Training Officer, Seán Murray.

On 25 February 1921, this column of some 60 men had a major engagement with the Auxilaries at Coolnacahera (sometimes erroneously referred to as the Coolavokig ambush). As well as the city contingent, men from Cill na Martra, Ballingeary, Ballyvourney and Macroom, i.e., the 2nd; 7th; and 8th Battalions were involved.

The column had left its billet in Cloontycarty early that morning, as it had done each day for a number of days previously to lie in ambush for Auxiliares from Macroom Castle heading for Ballyvourney. It crossed the Sullane at Tom Murray's steps and moved across country to take up position on both sides of the Ballyvourney road.

Following their mauling at Kilmichael a few months before, The Macroom Auxies now moved out only in large number and usually accompanied by hostages. On this day there were seven lorries of soldiers led by a touring car in which the Commander Major Seafield Grant travelled. The hostages were forced to walk ahead of the vehicles, a sign that the Auxies were expecting the ambush; the four hostages escaped when the shooting started.

The fight began around 8.00 a.m. and raged for over four hours. Children attending Ballyvoige NS in Cill na Martra village stood at the front gate listening to the firefight. In the course of the battle some 14 Auxilaries were killed, including the commanding officer Major Grant (shot by Cill na Martra Volunteer Mick 'the soldier' O'Connell- a World war I veteran and a marksman with a rifle- one of four O'Connell brothers who were active in the local IRA) and his second in command Lt. Sodie.

As a recent writer has noted, 'the ambush at Coolnacaheragh had the potential to have been a more spectacular action than Kilmichael.'[14] The Auxilaries would undoubtedly have been completely over-run except for the fact that Cruxy Connors – later unmasked as a British spy who a month later betrayed a group of Volunteers at Clogheen near Cork city leading to their torture and killing – who had one of the two Lewis guns in the column failed to fire it, falsely claiming it wouldn't work. This allowed the Auxilaries to clear the road and gain cover in and near two roadside cottages.

Following Clogheen, the British took Connors to London, but the IRA traced him there. He was then spirited to New York. However he had the bad luck of being spotted in the street one day by a woman from Cork. She got word back to the IRA. Brigade Intelligence Officer Florrie O'Donoghue recalled: 'At a time when every man and every shilling was needed, we went to the trouble and expense of sending three men after him to America'.[15] Pa Murray, a leading IRA man in Cork city and two other Volunteers shot him outside Central Park in April 1922. Michael Collins had sanctioned the mission. Connors had been an agent of Captain Kelly, Intelligence Officer of the British Army's 6th Division stationed at Victoria Barracks in Cork. Kelly was involved in the torture of many IRA prisoners, including Tom Hales. It was the attempted assassination of Kelly at the Dillon's Cross ambush which led to the burning of Cork city as a reprisal.[16]

At about noon a huge number of British reinforcements from Ballincollig and Cork approached from the east in 35 to 40 lorries. This forced the column to execute a fighting withdrawal to the north-west, to a pre-arranged assembly point at Coomnaclohy.

The No. 4 section of the ambush party (south of the road) apparently did not hear the order to withdraw and stayed in position for a while before realising what was happening. It was only when they heard shooting to the north-west as the IRA skirmished wth the advancing troop reinforcements that they realised the dangerous position they were in. Under renewed pressure from the Auxies and with the troops closing in, they too managed to make a successful fighting retreat without casualties and joined their comrades at Coomnaclohy.

The column had another narrow escape here when British troops from Killarney came upon them. Having inflicted two or three casualties on the British forces, the column again evaded their pursuers, their only casualty being a minor wound to one Volunteer.

Along with the troops from Ballincollig and Cork to the east and Killarney to the west, Auxilaries also came from Dunmanway to the south. The British had hoped to encircle the column and destroy it while it was engaging with the Macroom Auxilaries. Instead a serious defeat was inflicted on the British, with no losses to the IRA.

Shortly after the column's successful escape, the men returned to Cill na Martra and the surrounding district. Mick 'the soldier' was working for a local farmer, thinning turnips on Caherdaha hill when he was surprised by a party of Auxies. He was so engrossed in the work that he hadn't heard them approach as they came up the hill on foot ahead of their motor transport. As they came into the field he knew he was in trouble as he had Major Grant's watch, inscribed with the owner's name, in his possession. Thinking quickly, he scooped a hole in the earth and put the watch in it; he then put his knee on that spot and continued working. The Auxies questioned him about named Volunteers they were after (including himself!), but he kept on working with his head down and said he was just a travelling labourer hired by a local farmer and didn't know anyone in the district. Eventually the Auxies went back to the road and began to get into their lorries.

He was starting to relax when he suddenly heard a voice: 'How are you, Mick? I knew you the minute I walked into the field.' Looking up, he saw that one of the Auxies had returned. They had both been prisoners of war together in World War I. He thought he was finished but the Auxie told him: 'Don't worry,

I won't give you away.' The Auxie warned him that they knew he was at Coolnacahera and were anxious to catch him. 'If they catch you, you're a dead man', he warned. The Auxie then said he has better go or the others would start to get suspicious; he would tell them he had decided to question the labourer some more. He wished Mick good luck and told him to mind himself. He then left and the two never saw each other again.

The importance of Cill na Martra and other Battalions in the western part of the No.1 Brigade is shown by Major Florrie O'Donoghue's account of the attack on Blarney RIC post. He stated it was important for the Brigade to compel the evacuation of Blarney Barracks 'because it menaced one of the main lines of communication between Brigade Headquarters and the Sixth, Seventh and Eighth Battalions, with headquarters at Donoughmore, Macroom and Kilnamartyra respectively.'[17]

Local Volunteers were also involved in the ambush of a British raiding party at Knocksaharn and in the attack on Millstreet RIC Barracks.

Like the rest of the country, Cill na Martra divided during the Civil War, with some supporting the Free State and others supporting the Republicans. Jeremiah Murphy of Kilquane, Co. Kerry, in his memoir of those days tells us that he, along with other elements of the Kerry IRA, came over the mountains from the Kenmare area. They went through Renaniree, where their scouts exchanged fire with a Free State patrol. They joined with elements of the Cork IRA, including Volunteers from Cill na Martra for an attack on a Free State Headquarters, located at the hotel in Ballyvourney. This post had over 200 troops supported by an armoured car.

The IRA used the Sliabh na mBan armoured car, captured from Free Sate forces in Bandon by Tom Barry. Manned by Mick Sullivan, the Siabh na mBan gave the IRA the firepower to force the surrender of the Free State forces. This, along with the evacuation of the Inchigeelagh barracks left a 'large area from Kenmare to Macroom ... cleared of enemy garrisons and it was possibly to move around there without fear of running into patrols.'[18]

Notes and References

[1] *Cill na Martra*, p.43

[2] *ibid.*

[3] Quoted in David Dickson, *op. cit.*, p.177

[4] See Denis Paul Ring, *op. cit.*, p.132

[5] *Cill na Martra*, p.47

[6] Michael Galvin, *The Slow Sunrise: Land Reform*Labour*Home Rule in Mid Cork 1865-1881*, [n.d./publisher], p.261

[7] Micheál Ó Súilleabháin, *Where Mountainy Men Have Sown*, 1965, p.23

[8] *Lee Valley Outlook* 8 April 2004

[9] John Borgonovo (ed.), *Florence and Josephine O'Donoghue's War of Independence: A Destiny That Shapes Our Ends*, 2006, p.77

[10] Desmond Ryan, *Sean Treacy and the Third Tipperary Brigade I.R.A.*, 1945, p.50

[11] See T. Ryle Dwyer, *Tans, Terror and Troubles: Kerry's Real Fighting Story 1913-23*, 2001, p.126

[12] John Borgonovo, *Spies, Informers and the 'Anti-Sinn Féin Society': The Intelligence War in Cork City 1920-1921*, 2007, p.105

[13] Peter Hart, *The I.R.A. & Its Enemies: Violence and Community in Cork 1916-1923*, 1998, p.10

[14] Kevin Girvin, *Seán O'Hegarty: Officer Commanding, First Cork Brigade, Irish Republican Army*, 2007, p.77

[15] John Borgonovo (ed.), *op. cit.*, 2006, p.83

[16] Gerry White and Brendan O'Shea, *The Burning of Cork*, 2006, p.106

[17] F. O'Donoghue, 'The Attack on Blarney Police Barracks', 1947, p.39

[18] Jeremiah Murphy, *When Youth was Mine: A Memoir of Kerry 1902-1925*, 1998, p.235

CONCLUSION

On 21 December 1802 a Daniel O'Connell was born in Cill na Martra, probably somewhere along the main Bealach Feabhradh ridge as later documentation noted he was from near the 'village' of Macroom. He emigrated to America in 1851 as part of the post-Famine flight from the area and settled near Detroit, Michigan. He lived to the great age of 104 years and after he died in 1906 his headstone recorded he was from 'Tognadromun'.[1] The old name for the parish survived even in the New World. As William J. Smyth has said, 'the ghosts of the *tuatha* survived in the shape of the parishes.'[2]

It has been written in another context that there are two types of parishes in the country: 'those defined by mere boundaries and those defined by history...'[3] We have seen that Cill na Martra is of this latter type.

Notes and References

[1] www.freewebz.com/toomey/oconnellhistory.htm

[2] William J. Smyth, *Map-making, Landscapes and Memory: A Geography of Colonial and Early Modern Ireland c. 1530-1750*, 2006, p.84

[3] Diarmuid O'Flynn, *Club, Sweat and Tears: The Newtown Story*, 2006, p.2

BIBLIOGRAPHY

1. Barnard, Toby, *A Guide to Sources For The History of Material Culture in Ireland 1500-2000*, Maynooth Research Guides for Irish Local History, Four Courts Press, Dublin, 2005
2. Beaumont, Daniel, 'Greatrakes "the stroaker"', *History Ireland*, Jan/Feb, 2007
3. Bollando S.I., Ioanne, *Acta Sanctorum Martii*, Impression Anastaltique Culture et Civilisation, reprinted 1968
4. Borgonovo, John (ed.), *Florence and Josephine O'Donoghue's War Of Independence: A Destiny That Shapes Our Ends*, Irish Academic Press, Dublin, 2006
5. Borgonovo, John, *Spies, Informers and the "Anti-Sinn Féin Society": The Intelligence War in Cork City 1920-1921*, Irish Academic Press, Dublin, 2007
6. Brady, W. Maziere, *Clerical and Parochial Records of Cork, Cloyne and Ross*,
Vols. I and II, Alexander Thom, Dublin, 1863
Vol. III, Longman, Green, Roberts, Longman & Green, London, 1864
7. Breen, Colin, *The Gaelic Lordship of the O'Sullivan Beare: A Landscape Cultural History*, Four Courts Press, Dublin, 2005
8. Brennan, Brian, *Máire Bhuí Ní Laoire: A Poet of her People*, The Collins Press, Cork, 2000
9. Bromwich, Rachel, 'The Keen for Art O'Leary, Its background and Its Place in the Tradition of Gaelic Keening', *Éigse: A Journal of Irish Studies*, ed. Gerard Murphy, Vol. V, part IV, Winter 1947 (1948), pp. 236-52
10. Buckley, James, 'The Parish Priests of Counties Cork and Kerry in

1740'[sic], *Journal of the Cork Historical and Archaeological Society* [*JCHAS*], 45, 1900, pp. 55-60

11. Buckley, James, 'The Investiture of Donal MacCarthy Mór with the Earldom of Clancar, A.D. 1565', *Journal of the Waterford and South- East of Ireland Archaeological Society* [*JWSEIAS*], Vol. XI, 1908, pp.100-02

12. Buckley, James, 'Selections from a General Account Book of Valentine Greatrakes, A.D. 1663-1679', *JWSEIAS*, Vol. XI, 1908, pp. 211-24

13. Burl, Aubrey, *A Guide to the Stone Circles of Britain, Ireland and Brittany*, Yale University press, New Haven and London, 1995

14. Butler, William F.T., *Gleanings from Irish History*, Longmans, Green and Co., London, 1925

15. Byrne, Francis J., *Irish Kings and High-Kings*, Four Courts Press, Dublin, 2001, [first published London, 1973]

16. Byrne, Joseph, *Byrne's Dictionary of Irish Local History: from earliest times to c.1900*, Mercier Press, Cork, 2004

17. Cadogan, Tim and Jeremiah Falvey, *A Biographical Dictionary of Cork*, Four Courts Press, Dublin, 2006

18. Casey, Albert E., *O'Kief, Coshe Mang, Slieve Lougher and Upper Blackwater in Ireland*, 16 Vols., Birmingham, Alabama, 1952-71 [published privately]

19. Charles-Edwards, T.M., *Early Christian Ireland*, Cambridge University Press, Cambridge, 2000

20. *Cill na Martra: Muscraí Co. Chorcaí*, Coiste Forbartha [gan data]

21. Cobhar, 'Maoilsheachlainn Ó Dubhgáin', *An Músgraigheach*, 2, Fóghmhar 1943, pp.3-6

22. Coleman, J.C., *Journeys into Muskerry*, Dundalgan Press, Dundalk [n.d.]

23. Collins, John T., 'Fiants of Queen Elizabeth relating to City and County of Cork: with notes', *JCHAS*, XLIII, 1938, pp.12-20; XLVII, 1942, pp. 34-42; LIII, 1948, pp. 95-103

24. Connolly, Philomena, *Medieval Record Sources,* Maynooth Research Guides for Irish Local History, Four Courts Press, Dublin, 2002

25. Coombes, Rev. James, 'Catholic Churches of the Nineteenth Century:

Some Newspaper Sources', *JCHAS*, LXXXI, 1975, pp.1-12

26. Day, Robert, 'First Muskerry Cavalry. Notes from the Orderly Book of the First Troop of the Muskerry Legion of Yeomanry Cavalry, 1796, with reduced facsimile page of Orderly Book', *JCHAS*, II, 1896, pp.1-10

27. de Blácam, Aodh, *Cúltroid Uí Shúileabháin Bhéara: The Great Retreat*, Cló Duanaire, Cork, 1987

28. Dickson, David, *Old World Colony: Cork and South Munster 1630-1830*, Cork University Press, Cork, 2005

29. *Diocese of Cloyne 2002: A glimpse of our Christian Heritage*, Editions du Signe, Strasbourg, France, 2002

30. Dwyer, T. Ryle, *Tans, Terror and Troubles: Kerry's Real Fighting Story 1913-1923*, Mercier Press, Cork, 2001

31. Edwards, Nancy, *The Archaeology of Early Medieval Ireland*, Batsford, London, 1990

32. Emerson, Lucius J., *The March of O'Sullivan Beare*, [no publisher or date given]

33. Etchingham, Colmán, *Church Organisation in Ireland AD 650 to 1000*, Laigin Publications, Maynooth, 1999

34. Etchingham, Colmán, 'Pastoral provision in the first millennium: a two-tier service?' in Elizabeth FitzPatrick and Raymond Gillespie (eds.), *The Parish in Medieval and Early Modern Ireland: Community, Territory and Building*, Four Courts Press, Dublin, 2006, pp.79-90

35. Farrar, Henry, *Irish Marriages: Being an Index to the Marriages in Walker's Hibernian Magazine 1771 to 1812*, London, 1890

36. Fitzpatrick, Benedict, *Ireland and the Foundations of Europe*, Funk & Wagnalls Company, New York and London, 1927

37. FitzPatrick, Elizabeth, *Royal Inauguration in Gaelic Ireland c.1100-1600: A Cultural Landscape Study*, The Boydell Press, Woodbridge, 2004

38. Gabriel, Brian, 'Times Past: St. Laichtin's and St. Ann's Wells ', *Muskerry News* March 2006

39. Galvin, Michael, *The Slow Sunrise:Land Reform*Labour*Home Rule in Mid Cork 1865-1881* [no date or publisher given]

40. Girvin, Kevin, *Seán O'Hegarty: Officer Commanding, First Cork Brigade, Irish Republican Army*, Aubane Historical Society, Millstreet, 2007

41. Hart, Peter, *The I.R.A. & Its Enemies: Violence and Community in Cork 1916-1923*, Clarendon Press, Oxford, 1998

42. Hayman B.A., Rev. Samuel, 'Notes On the family of Greatrakes', *Reliquary Quarterly Archaeological Journal*, XIV, 1863

43. Haywood, John, *The Celts: Bronze Age to New Age*, Pearson Longman, Harlow, 2004

44. Healy, James N., *Castles of County Cork*, Mercier Press, Cork, 1988

45. Herbert, Máire, 'Ireland and Scotland: The Foundations of a Relationship' in Gordon McCoy, Maolcholaim Scott (eds.), *Aithne na nGael: Gaelic Identities*, Institute of Irish Studies/ Iontabhas Ultach, Belfast, 2000

46. Hogan S.J., Edmund, *Onamasticon Goedelicum: Locorum et Tribuum Hiberniae et Scotiae*, Hodges Figgis, Dublin and Williams and Norgate, London, 1910

47. Kennan, Pádhraig S., *Written in Stone*, Geological Survey of Ireland, 1995

48. Kenney, J.F., *Sources for the early history of Ireland: 1 ecclesiastical*, New York, 1929

49. *Lee Valley Outlook* 8 April 2004

50. Lewis, Samuel, *Lewis' Cork: A Topographical Dictionary of the Parishes and Villages of Cork City and County*, The Collins Press, 1998 [first published 1837]

51. Lyons, John, 'Local Names. Topographical and Personal', *JCHAS*, III, 1894, pp.132-33

52. Lyons, Patrick, 'How Kilnamartyra Got Its Name', *Cork Examiner* 1 January 1941

53. MacAirt, Seán (ed.), *The Annals of Inisfallen (Ms. Rawlinson B. 503)*, Dublin Institute for Advanced Studies, 1988 [first published 1944]

54. MacBain, Alexander, *An Etymological Dictionary of the Gaelic Language*, first ed. 1896; second ed. 1911; Photolithic Reprint of 1911 ed.

By Gairm Publications, Glasgow, 1982

55. McCarthy, C.J.F., 'Baldwins Hold Lot of Kilnamartyra', *Southern Star* 1 August 1970

56. McCarthy, C.J.F., 'History of Kilnamartyra Parish-3: Local Connections with St Lachtin', *Southern Star* 15 August 1970

57. McCoole, Sinead, 'The Herberts of Muckross' in Jim Larner (ed.), *Killarney: History and Heritage*, the Collins Press, Cork, 2005, pp.90-104

58. MacCotter, Paul and Nicholls, Kenneth (eds.), *The Pipe Roll of Cloyne (Rotulus Pipae Clonensis)*, Cloyne Literary and Historical Society, Midleton, 1996

59. MacKillop, James, *Myths and Legends of the Celts*, Penguin Books, London, 2005

60. MacSuibhne, Dáithi agus Seán (cnuasaitheoirí), *Slí na Staire i gCill na Martra: Historical Byways*, Coiste Forbartha Chill na Martra, 2006

61. MacSuibhne, Máire, *Famine in Muskerry: an Drochshaol*, Litho Press, Midleton, Co. Cork, 1997

62. Michelli, Perette E., 'Fragments of a fifth crosier from Scotland', *Proc. Soc. Antiq. Scot.*, 118 (1988), pp.215-18

63. Michelli, Perette E., 'The Inscriptions on pre-Norman Irish Reliquaries', *Proceedings of the Royal Irish Academy*, 96C, 1996, pp.1-18

64. Mitchell, G.F., 'The Cap of St. Lachtin's Arm', *Journal of the Royal Society of Antiquaries of Ireland*, 114 (1984), pp.139-40

65. Mould, Daphne D.C., *Discovering Cork*, Brandon Books, Dingle, 1991

66. Mulligan, Paul, *A Short Guide to Irish Antiquities*, Wordwell, Bray, 2005

67. Murphy, Conor, 'Parish of Cill-na-Martra; Its Ancient Topography and Traditions- Part I', *JCHAS*, III, 1897, pp. 275-90; Part II, *JCHAS*, IV, 1898, pp.1-19

68. Murphy, Jeremiah, *When Youth Was Mine: A Memoir of Kerry 1902-1925*, MENTOR Press, Dublin, 1998

69. Murray, Griffin, 'The Arm-Shaped Reliquary of St. Lachtin: Technique,

Style and Significance', in Colum Hourihane (ed.), *Irish Art Historical Studies in honour of Peter Harbison*, Four Courts Press, Dublin, 2004, pp.141-64

70. 'Músgraighe Uí Fhloinn', *An Músgraigheach*, 1, Meitheamh 1943, lch.4-5 [gan údar luaite]

71. Nicholls, Kenneth (ed.), *The Irish Fiants of the Tudor Sovereigns: During the reigns of Henry VIII, Edward VI, Philip and Mary and Elizabeth I*, Edmund Burke, Dublin, 1994, 4 Vols.

72. Nicholls, K.W., *Gaelic and Gaelicized Ireland in the Middle Ages*, Lilliput Press, Dublin, 2003 [first published 1971]

73. O'Brien, Barry, *Macroom: A Chronicle*, No.1, 1990 [no publisher given]

74. Ó Buachalla, Breandán, 'The Making of a Cork Jacobite' in Patrick O'Flanagan & Cornelius Buttimer (eds), *Cork: History & Society*, Geography Publications, Dublin, 1993, pp.469-97

75. Ó Cróinín, Dáibhí, *Early Medieval Ireland: 400-1200*, Longman, London and New York, 1995

76. Ó Cuív, Brian, *Catalogue of Irish Language Manuscripts in the Bodleian Library at Oxford and Oxford College Libraries, Part 1 Descriptions*, School of Celtic Studies, Dublin Institute for Advanced Studies, Dundalgan Press, Dundalk, 2001; *Part 2 Plates and Indexes*, 2003

77. O'Curry, Eugene, *Lectures on the Manuscript Materials of Ancient Irish History*, James Duffy, Dublin & London, 1861

78. Ó Donnchadha, Tadhg, *An Leabhar Muimhneach*, Coimisiún Láimhscríbhinní na hÉireann, Dublin, 1940

79. O'Donoghue, Bruno, *Parish Histories and Place Names of West Cork*, Kerryman Ltd., Tralee, 1983

80. O'Donoghue, F., 'The Attack on Blarney Police Barracks' in *Rebel Cork's Fighting Story 1916-21: Told by the Men Who Made It*, The Kerryman Ltd., Tralee, 1947, pp.39-42

81. O'Donovan, John (ed.), *Annála Ríoghachta Éireann; Annals of the Kingdom of Ireland*, second ed., Hodges, Smith, and Co., Dublin, 1856

82. Seán Ó Duinn (trans.), *Forbhais Droma Dámhghaire: The Siege of Knocklong*, Mercier Press, Cork, 1992

83. Ó Floinn, Raghnall, *Irish Shrines and Reliquaries of the Middle Ages*, National Museum of Ireland, Dublin, 1994

84. O'Flynn, Diarmuid, *Club, Sweat and Tears: The Newtown Story*, The Collins Press, Cork, 2006

85. O'Hart, John, *Irish Pedigrees: or The Origin & Stem of the Irish Nation*, Vols I & II, P. Murphy & Son, New York, 1915 [first published 1875]

86. O'Hanlon, Very Rev. John Canon, *Lives of the Irish Saints: with special festivals, and the commemorations of the holy persons compiled from calendars, martyrologies, and various sources, relating to the ancient church history of Ireland*, 10 Vols., James Duffy and Sons, Dublin; Burns, Oates & Co., London; Catholic Publishing Society, New York, 1875-1903

87. O'Kelly, Michael J., *Early Ireland: An Introduction to Irish Prehistory*, Cambridge University Press, 1989

88. Ó Laoghaire, An t-Athair Peadar, *Mo Scéal Féin*, Longmans, Brún agus Ó Nualláin Tta., Baile Átha Cliath [gan dáta]

89. O'Leary, Peter, 'The Life and times of Art Ó Laoghaire', *Ballingeary History Society*, 1998

90. O'Mahony, Colman, *Cork's Poor Law Palace: Workhouse Life 1838-90*, Rosmathún Press, Co. Cork, 2005

91. O'Mahony, Jeremiah, *West Cork: Parish Histories and Place Names*, The Kerryman Ltd., Tralee [n.d.]

92. O'Mahony, Jeremiah, *West Cork: and Its Story*, The Kerryman Ltd., Tralee [n.d.]

93. O'Mahony, Michelle, *Famine in Cork City*, Mercier Press, Cork, 2005

94. Ó Maidín, Pádraig, 'A Parish Priest of Macroom', *Cork Examiner* 16 October 1968

95. Ó Maidín, P., 'Death of Art Ó Laoghaire', *Cork Examiner* 4 May 1970

96. Ó Maidín, P., 'Aftermath to Battle of Keimaneigh', *Cork Examiner* 23 February 1971

97. Ó Maidín, P., 'A battle near Macroom in 1822', *Cork Examiner* 24

January 1972

98. Ó Maidín, P., 'A lively Cork meeting of 1837', *Cork Examiner* 3 May 1972

99. Ó Maidín, P., 'The O'Herlihy's of Ballyvourney', *Cork Examiner* 9 May 1972

100. Ó Máille, T.S., 'Irish Place-Names ending in *–AS, -ES, -IS, OS, -US* ', *AINM Bulletin of the Ulster Place-Name Society*, IV, 1989-90, pp.125-43

101. Ó Maolfabhail, Art, 'Baill Choirp mar Logainmneacha', *AINM*, II, 1997, pp.76-82; *AINM*, III, 1988, pp.18-25

102. Ó Murchadha, Diarmuid, 'The Uí Mhurchadha or Murphys of Muskerry, Co. Cork', *JCHAS*, LXXIV, 1969, pp.1-19

103. Ó Murchadha, D., *Family Names of County Cork*, Glendale Press, Dun Laoghaire, 1985

104. Ó Murchadha, D., 'Gaelic land Tenure in County Cork: Uíbh Laoghaire in the Seventeenth Century' in Patrick O'Flanagan & Cornelius Buttimer (eds.), *Cork: History & Society: Interdisciplinary Essays on the History of an Irish County*, Geography Publications, Dublin, 1993, pp.213-48

105. Ó Riain, Pádraig, 'Traces of Lug in early Irish hagiographical tradition', *Zeitschrift fur Celtische Philologie*, 1978, pp.138-56

106. Ó Riain-Raedel, Dagmar, 'A German visitor to Monaincha in 1591', *Tipperary Historical Journal*, 1998, pp.223-33

107. Ó Riordáin, Seán P., *Antiquities of the Irish Countryside*, Methuen, London and New York, 1987 [first published 1942]

108. Ó Súilleabháin, Micheál, *Where Mountainy Men Have Sown*, Anvil Books, Tralee, 1965

109. Ó Tuama, Seán, *Caoineadh Airt Uí Laoghaire*, An Clóchomhar Tta., Baile Átha Cliath, 1961 [athchló 1979]

110. P., 'Extracts from an Antiquary's Note Book', *JWSEIAS*, 13, 1910, PP.17-167

111. Power, Denis, with Elizabeth Byrne, Ursula Egan, Sheila Lane, Mary Sleeman. *Archaeological Inventory of County Cork: Vol. 3: Mid Cork*, Stationery Office, Dublin, 1997

112. Ring, Denis Paul, *Macroom Through the Mists of Time: An Historical*

Geography of Macroom c.500-1995, Castle House Publications, Carrigadrohid, Macroom, 1995

113. Roberts, Jack, *Exploring West Cork: The Guide to Discovering the Ancient, Sacred and Historic Sites*, Key Books, Skibbereen, 1988

114. Ryan, Desmond, *Sean Treacy and the Third Tipperary Brigade I.R.A.*, Anvil Books, Tralee, 1945

115. Rynne, Colin, 'Early Medieval Horizontal-Wheeled Mill Penstocks from Co. Cork', *JCHAS*, 97, 1992, pp.54-67

116. Rynne, Colin, 'Horizontal Mills in Mediaeval Ireland', *Transactions of the Newcomen Society*, 70:2, 1998-99,pp.251-55

117. Simington, Robert C., *The Civil Survey AD 1654-1656 County of Waterford Vol. VI with appendices: Muskerry Barony, Co. Cork: Kilkenny City and Liberties (Part) also Valuations, circa 1663-64, for Waterford and Cork Cities*, Coimisiún Láimhscríbhinní na hÉireann, Stationery Office, Dublin, 1942

118. Slavin, Michael, *The Ancient Books of Ireland*, Wolfhound Press, Dublin, 2005

119. Smith M.D., Charles, *The Ancient and Present State of the County and City of Cork*, second ed., Cork, 1815

120. Smyth, William J., *Map-making, Landscapes and Memory: A Geography of Colonial and Early Modern Ireland c.1530 1750*, Cork University Press/ Field Day, Cork, 2006

121. Stringer, Keith J., 'Reform Monasticism and Celtic Scotland : Galloway, c.1140-c.1240' in E.J. Cowen and R. Andrew McDonald (eds.), *Alba: Celtic Scotland in the Medieval Era*, John Donald, Edinburgh, 2005, pp.127-165

122. Toner, Gregory, 'The Backward Nook: *Cúil and Cúl in Irish Place-Names*', *AINM*, VII, 1996-7, pp.113-17

123. Twohig, Elizabeth Shee, *Irish Megalithic Tombs*, Shire Publications, Buckinghamshire, 2004 [second ed., first publ. 1990]

124. Ua Súilleabháin, Seán, 'Baile Bhúirne, Cill na Martra agus Cluain Droichead Múscraí' in Gearóid Ó Tuathaigh, Liam Lillis Ó Laoire, Seán Ua Súilleaháin (eag.), *Pobal na Gaeltachta: a scéal agus a dhán*, Cló Iar-

Chonnachta, Indreabhán, Conamara, 2000, pp. 653-75

125. Viney, Michael, *Ireland: A Smithsonian Natural History*, Blackstaff Press, Belfast, 2003

126. Wallace, Patrick F. and Ó Floinn, Raghnall, *Treasures of the National Museum of Ireland*, Gill and Macmillan, Dublin, 2002

127. Walsh, Paul, *Irish Leaders and Learning through the Ages*, ed. Nollaig Ó Muraíle, Four Courts Press, Dublin, 2003

128. White, Gerry and O'Shea, Brendan, *The Burning of Cork*, Mercier Press, Cork, 2006